ADHD PARENTING BIBLE

MINDFUL TECHNIQUES FOR RAISING HYPERACTIVE KIDS WITH BEHAVIORAL ISSUES. AN EFFECTIVE GUIDE TO PREVENT OUTBURST BY TEACHING EMOTIONAL SELF-CONTROL TO EXPLOSIVE CHILDREN

LINA COLE

Copyright © 2022 Lina Cole. All rights reserved.

The content contained within this book may not be reproduced, duplicated or transmitted without direct written permission from the author or the publisher.

Under no circumstances will any blame or legal responsibility be held against the publisher, or author, for any damages, reparation, or monetary loss due to the information contained within this book. Either directly or indirectly. You are responsible for your own choices, actions, and results.

Legal Notice:

This book is copyright protected. This book is only for personal use. You cannot amend, distribute, sell, use, quote or paraphrase any part, or the content within this book, without the consent of the author or publisher.

Disclaimer Notice:

Please note the information contained within this document is for educational and entertainment purposes only. All effort has been executed to present accurate, up to date, and reliable, complete information. No warranties of any kind are declared or implied. Readers acknowledge that the author is not engaging in the rendering of legal, financial, medical, or professional advice. The content within this book has been derived from various sources. Please consult a licensed professional before attempting any techniques outlined in this book.

By reading this document, the reader agrees that under no circumstances is the author responsible for any losses, direct or indirect, which are incurred as a result of the use of the information contained within this document, including, but not limited to, errors, omissions, or inaccuracies.

CONTENTS

About the Author   9
Introduction   11

1. UNDERSTANDING ADHD   19
   What is ADHD?   21
   Types Of ADHD   24
   Signs And Symptoms Of ADHD   28
   Causes Of ADHD   28
   Diagnosis of ADHD   30
   When Both Parents Have ADHD   31

2. CHALLENGES OF PARENTING AN ADHD KID   37
   Parental Challenges   40
   Kids And Bad behavior   45
   Is It Really ADHD?   47
   Coping With ADHD Stigma   50

3. EXECUTIVE FUNCTION 101   55
   Signs of Executive Dysfunction   57
   Stress and Executive Function   58
   Stress VS. Executive function   58
   Strategies to Reduce Stress With ADHD   60
   Executive Function and Brain Development   62
   Strategies to Improve Executive Function   64
   Age-Appropriate Activities to Improve Executive Function in Kids   67

4. ADHD AND ADOLESCENCE   77
   ADHD Symptoms In Teens.   79
   Teen Gender & ADHD   81

Common Challenges Of Teens With ADHD	83
Diagnosing ADHD In Teens	85
Parenting Strategies For Teens With ADHD	87
Strategies For Building Teen Executive Function	91
Activities For Executive Functioning In Teens	94
5. THERE'S A PROBLEM. WHAT'S THE SOLUTION?	99
Possible Treatment Options for ADHD	101
Side Effects of Medication	103
What Causes Side Effects?	105
Golden Rules For ADHD Medications	106
Parent Training & Education Programs	109
Social Skills Training	110
Health & Diet For Kids With ADHD	111
Nutrients & Supplements For ADHD	113
Elimination Diet For ADHD	115
6. HANDLING THE EMOTIONAL DISTRESS	117
Coping Strategies	119
ADHD & Emotions	124
Golden Rules For Enhancing Emotion Control	126
ADHD & Anger – the connection between the two	126
Moodiness and Mood Disorders	127
ODD aka Oppositional Defiant Disorder	128
Symptoms of Emotional Distress	130
The Link Between ADHD and Childhood Trauma	131
Shared ADHD & Childhood Trauma Symptoms	132

Childhood Trauma vs ADHD: Case Study	133
How to Help Your Child Overcome Trauma & Strengthen Emotional Regulation	134
7. NURTURING SELF-ESTEEM	**141**
Self-Esteem In Children	143
What Causes Low Self-Esteem in Children?	148
Narcissism and ADHD… and some thoughts on damage repair	150
How Narcissism Affects ADHD Kids	153
Coping Strategies For Coping With A Narcissistic Parent	154
8. HANDLING THE WRECKING BALL	**161**
Behavior Problems & ADHD Children	163
Coping Strategies for Disruptive Behaviour	174
Encourage Honesty	174
Extinguishing Deliberate Lies	175
Truth Check	177
Preamble Method	177
Turning Defiance into Healthy Compliance	178
Parental Tools & Apps	181
Clarify behavioral expectations	185
Code words	189
9. SOME LESSONS IN MANNERS	**191**
Importance of Good Manners	193
Why teaching good manners to kids is essential	194
Tips & Strategies For Good Role Model Behavior	196
What Not To Do	199
When Your Kids Won't Listen	201
Why don't kids listen?	202

Tips to encourage kids to listen	203
Activities That Teach Good Values	206

10. HELL, DON'T YELL! — 211
- Parenting Pitfalls — 213
- Yelling is not a solution — 218
- Anger management tips for parents — 219
- Forging better relationships — 224
- Teaching empathy to your kids — 227

11. COLLABORATING WITH SCHOOLS — 231
- Role of Schools — 233
- How can teachers help kids with ADHD? — 234
- How can parents collaborate with teachers to help kids? — 240
- Tips for making learning fun — 241
- Tips for managing ADHD symptoms at school — 243
- What parents should know — 246
- How teachers can help — 248

12. THE SELF-LOVING PARENT — 253
- The importance of self-care — 255
- How does self-care benefit parenting? — 256
- Practicing self-care strategies for parents — 258

13. NO MAN IS AN ISLAND — 269
- Support for parents — 270
- Types of support — 271
- Joining a support group — 274
- Types of support groups — 277
- How to find a support group near you — 279

Conclusion — 283
Resources Page — 291

JUST FOR YOU!

A FREE GIFT TO OUR READERS

Tantrum Soothers

Simply scan the QR code below
to request access to this FREE resource!

ABOUT THE AUTHOR

Lina Cole is your average down to earth Mom, focused like you on providing the best possible loving environment and care for her children. She has spent years wading through the isolating quagmire of the ADHD parenting warzone before diving into writing **parenting books**.

From deep within the murky ADHD trenches, Lina understands the stressful situations you face caused by your child's incorrectly assumed 'bad' behavior! While she doesn't have University degrees as long as her arm or titles to match, her practical parenting tips for **calm parenting** are formulated and based on 21 years of hard-grafting experience. Raising kids with ADHD is fraught with tantrums, outbursts, and ODD, you name it; Lina has faced it head-on and often alone.

Mother to an ADHD child, only officially diagnosed as an adult, 21 years later, Lina has undoubtedly earned her proverbial stripes and understands the struggles ADHD parents face. ADHD Parenting Bible is a practical, no-nonsense guide to effectively raising explosive ADHD kids in a loving environment. Forget unrealistic **ADHD parenting books**, backed by mind-numbing sciency fluff as Lina Cole gets to the heart of the matter and teaches you how to calm the raging tide that has washed over your home, life, and happiness.

In the words of Lina Cole, ADHD might feel like a battle, but it's not the final battle. Although it feels like every skirmish requires full-combat gear right now, you will discover how to dodge those firebombs that strike on 'down' days and develop a **calm ADHD** co-existence with your beautiful child.

If you are ready to combat the chaos that currently rules your home, join her Jodi call, grab your combat boots and helmet; it's time to dive into the ADHD warzone and initiate operation peace be still!

INTRODUCTION

"Don't be afraid to ask for help and to admit when you need it."

— CHARLES SCHWAB

Sitting on the top step of the garden stairs, I can vaguely hear the screaming, kicking, and yelling coming from my son's bedroom. It's your average Saturday morning for most families, except ours. Instead of sunny smiles around the breakfast table, while chatting and eagerly anticipating the day, an entire carton of orange juice is spread across the floor. A smashed coffee cup decorates the wall, and a plate of cold toast with runny egg congealing on the side lies forgotten in the middle of the table—the evidence of my impromptu cooked breakfast. I should have known better and stuck to the cereal eaten every morning 365 days of the year.

I have my back to the kitchen door as I sit on the steps, but if I glance slightly to the left, I can just about see the overturned coffee table, broken lampshade, and my antique flower vase lying on its side; the flowers dangling drunkenly to one side as the water pools on the rug.

I'm sitting here not because I'm ignoring my son's obvious distress but because I'm struggling to breathe. No, I'm not hurt, well, not physically anyway, but the pain in my chest is threatening to drown me. As I gasp for air, trying to calm myself, the cool air from the garden doesn't seem to want to be absorbed by my desperate lungs. The sweat drips down my back, and that ever-present voice in my head says in its rather sneery voice, 'see, you failed again, you always do!'

At this point, I'm sure you are probably wondering what on earth could have happened. A burglary? Or perhaps a classic case of domestic violence? However, you would be wrong on both counts. We have an excellent intruder alarm, and my hubby is a loving spouse. No, unfortunately, this is simply a day in the life of me,

Lina Cole. The warzone you just witnessed is a standard Saturday morning in our household as we prepare for a leisurely stroll in the market.

I say leisurely, but it's generally filled with tugging, pulling, pushing, and I'm ashamed to say, a lot of shouting - by me. Yes, I am the mom; you can hear shouting in the shops, screaming across the street, and yelling on the beach. Sound familiar? If not, before you judge me, there's a little something you should know.

I am the mother of two gorgeous boys, one of whom has ADHD. If you're reading this book, you either suspect your child or someone else has the same condition. Lucky for you, you seem to have twigged a lot sooner than I did. My son was only officially diagnosed with ADHD in adulthood, which means it was literally years before I finally understood the situation.

ADHD is a scary concept the first time you stare it in the proverbial eye, causing you to hide behind the cozy wall of denial. Ask yourself the following questions:

- Do you find it hard to keep calm when dealing with your kid?
- Do you have to constantly resort to using force or yelling to make your kid listen?
- Do you feel you are a lousy parent and unable to provide the support your kid needs?

- Are family members (siblings) struggling to deal with your child's distressing behavior?

If you answer yes to these questions, then ADHD is possibly on the cards. Unfortunately, there isn't a simple tick list to diagnose ADHD as it presents in several ways. But I'll dip into symptoms and diagnosis later in the book. The critical thing to grasp at this point is that you are not alone. There are quite a few of us in the leaky ADHD boat, manically rowing towards a better future for our kids.

The truth is more than 6 million children in the US suffer from ADHD, and this has increased exponentially over the past decade.

In my experience, not knowing was probably what compounded the problem and caused me to believe I was a terrible parent and shouldn't have had kids in the first place. In the spirit of honesty, I will confess that there were, and I'm embarrassed to say, still are times when I secretly wish I had been one of those people that declare 'I'm never having kids!' Aah, theirs must be a life of peace, but then I look at my beautiful boys and realize I wouldn't change them for the world.

As a parent, I'm sure you will agree that your goal in life is quite simple. Firstly, to be the greatest parent known to man, and secondly, to help your kids live the best lives possible. While the first may be a little hard to achieve, seeing as you are human and not a superhero with a penchant for lycra, the second is one all parents strive to achieve. There's nothing better than seeing your kids achieve their goals, and that starts with their first step, word, school, and job.

In fact, throughout their lives, you want them to be everything you never could and achieve everything you never did. But I don't need to tell you this. It's a parent thing that is somehow triggered the very first time you hold that tiny bundle in your arms.

In all their tiny glory, they represent potential. The potential to live a great life and ADHD doesn't have to be the reason why they don't! There I said it. But before you gasp at my audacity, let me go one step further. Your child is an amazing, extraordinary human being with the potential to achieve anything they desire. We as parents are here to help them do that, even if it feels as though you would rather hide in the kitchen cupboard quaffing a large 9 am glass of wine. Just kidding, but sometimes, okay, most times, parenting a child with ADHD can leave you feeling extremely overwhelmed.

That's why I've put this book together to help you understand the mystery of ADHD while avoiding unnecessary struggles, much like the ones I experienced because of not knowing.

If your parenting experience has been fraught with stressful situations caused by your child's seemingly negative behavior, please continue to read this book. I may not be an expert, with university degrees and long titles after my name, but I have more than 21 years of hard-grafting experience.

Between these pages, you won't find any unrealistic parenting ideas backed by sciency gurus who haven't experienced the full force of an ADHD tantrum or the exhaustion of yet another ruined family get-together. Instead, you will find a guide on calming the veritable storm that has become your life. My practical parenting tips for kids with ADHD will help you create the calm, peaceful and loving family environment you've been striving for.

If you think that you have already read all the books there are to read on this subject, think again. Yes, you have probably also spent many nights trawling YouTube and other parenting sites for information, but was any of it useful? Unfortunately, most information on ADHD is terribly boring to read and, at times, *very* outdated (sorry, but it's true!) – the information I will share with you is new, fresh, and informative.

My personal feeling is that living with ADHD is like living in a war zone; without any tactical knowledge, it's not going to end well! Furthermore, doing it alone and not asking for help is like trying to sneak across no man's land; you are sure to snag a tripwire or two! But perhaps you would rather do things at speed? Sadly, rushing full tilt towards the finishing line is also bound to set off a few landmines.

So, take it from someone who knows, someone who is still very much digging alongside you in the trenches – it will get better once you discover how to manage and live with ADHD rather than fighting it all the way. You're already halfway to a better life; having recognized your need for help, keep going.

So, if you are ready to roll up your sleeves, pull on your helmet and combat boots, then it's time to discover how to manage and live with ADHD minus the frustration that's filled your life for so long! Say goodbye to the warzone and hello to a new and fresh calmer life, the perfect environment to raise your beautiful child.

1

UNDERSTANDING ADHD

"Just because you don't understand it, doesn't mean it isn't so."

— ANONYMOUS

Getting to grips with ADHD, in the beginning, can be somewhat daunting. On top of grappling with this rather complex condition, every parent gets that sinking feeling when faced with 'there's something wrong with my kid!' Usually, this is compounded by the negative thought that our kids will be 'labeled' (horrible words). After all, life is hard enough without a label to follow them around! And for the most part, I can understand your concern; I've walked that road too.

However, I have learned that thoughts such as these prevent us from seeking the help we need. Which simply makes the ADHD road much more challenging and its journey that much more difficult. Furthermore, ADHD doesn't have to be the negative 'label' you envision!

With that in mind, my mission is to de-demonize ADHD and reveal it for what it truly is. Not the bogey man hiding in the closet or under the bed but a condition that, if understood, can be managed effectively, allowing your child to progress and flourish in the way God intended.

Firstly, let's take a look at some of the shocking facts surrounding ADHD:

- Research suggests that approximately 6.4 million kids between the ages of 4-17 in the US alone have been diagnosed with ADHD.
- Around 23% of the diagnosed children aren't receiving any form of medication or treatment for ADHD.
- Kids with ADHD may have other conditions like anxiety, depression, and stress, making their lives more difficult.

The truth is this condition is relatively common in the US, but that doesn't make it any easier to deal with. Even more concerning is that boys are more likely to be diagnosed with ADHD than girls – why you ask? The answer is simple. Boys with ADHD are more hyperactive (most of the time!) than girls with the same condition. As a result, they may 'act out' or cause problems in the home or classroom, leading to them being diagnosed with ADHD.

In contrast, girls with ADHD often fall below the ADHD radar, and it's only in their teens, when they struggle with things like depression, anxiety, or panic disorders, that ADHD is suddenly considered.

Now that you've had a moment to digest these cold hard facts let's dive into the world of ADHD and 'tease' it out a little to understand it better.

WHAT IS ADHD?

ADHD, also known as Attention-Deficit Hyperactivity Disorder, is a common behavioral condition that affects many children and adults. People who have this condition struggle to concentrate, appear agitated or restless, and act on impulse without considering things like consequence or rationale.

Of course, the above definition is the sciency one, which I am sure you have across in different variations on the internet. To be honest, I found these to be entirely superfluous and disconnected from my personal experience with ADHD. I needed something tangible to measure against my son's situation to make sense of it all, and I am sure you do too. Hopefully, my below anecdote will help you see how ADHD might apply to your child.

Example:

Rio is a lovely 5-year-old boy from Albuquerque, New Mexico. His family is large, busy, and very active. Rio, however, is quieter than his siblings and prefers his own company on the playground. His teachers have mentioned that he seems to daydream a lot and is easily distracted during lessons. Unfortunately, Rio is also often late with his homework and tends to leave it to the last minute.

His mother, Anna, often complains about Rio's absent-mindedness at home. She finds it extremely frustrating that she has to remind him multiple times to complete simple tasks, some as trivial as brushing his teeth. This is very exhausting for his mother, as she has to deal with this unnecessary stress while handling her work-life balance.

As parents, reminding our kids to do things is part of the job description. But when you become the proverbial broken record, perhaps it's time to step back and look at the situation from another angle.

You might say all kids are bored at school at some point, and you would be right. However, ADHD is more than just a little boredom. It's struggling to remember simple instructions or pay attention to detail.

Often people with ADHD cannot focus on instructions even when they are being directly spoken to. I've often thought this must feel similar to speaking in a foreign language. If you don't understand what the person is saying, you won't react appropriately. Those struggling with ADHD may hear your words (for the most part), but the link between what they mean and the subsequent action that needs to take place is missing.

This can be highly frustrating for the person passing on the instruction or request as they struggle to get the proper reaction – teeth brushed, homework completed. As a result, the frustration causes the tense and chaotic ADHD world you currently live in.

TYPES OF ADHD

ADHD presents in three ways: inattentive, hyperactive-impulsive, and combined presentation. Typically, ADHD is diagnosed according to the symptoms displayed over a period of six months. This may seem like a long time, but as a standard, it ensures that the correct diagnosis is applied and provided with the proper support and treatment.

- **Predominantly inattentive presentation**

This form of ADHD affects focus, concentration, and attention span. So often, those with inattentive ADHD are initially thought to be careless or lazy. But this couldn't be further from the truth.

Think about how you would feel if, when presented with a task, you found you couldn't hear the instructions properly? Not that inattentive ADHD is associated with being hard of hearing, but perhaps if you think of it like this.

Standing under the shower, the water rushing, the shower pump going, there's a lot of noise in the bathroom. If someone speaks to you through the bathroom door while the shower is going, can you hear them?

Possibly, but indistinctly. If, like me, you find yourself shouting back in frustration because you can't quite make out what they are saying, you are not alone. Why do kids always need you when you are covered in soap suds? I'm sure something in the soap triggers them to do this!

The other way to handle this type of situation is to block out what the person on the other side of the bathroom door is saying. After all, I can't hear them anyway, and hopefully, the house fire will hold off long enough for me to rinse my hair. Just kidding,

But, my point is kids with inattentive ADHD hear but don't hear. Eventually, after struggling to decipher the message and coming up with nothing, they zone out, and that's where the broken record issues begin.

Symptoms:

◇ Struggles to focus on activities / tasks (lectures,conversations,reading)
◇ Appears not to listen
◇ Does not follow instructions easily
◇ Very disorganized (schoolwork, time management, messy)
◇ Avoids tasks that require mental effort
◇ Often misplaces personal items (books, toys, keys)

⋄ Forgets daily chores/tasks (homework, teeth cleaning)
⋄ Doesn't pay attention to detail and makes careless mistakes
⋄ Is easily distracted

- **Predominantly hyperactive-impulsive presentation**

Hyperactive-impulsive ADHD is what I call the 'busy' form of ADHD. This is when the symptoms of ADHD are more movement-related or, for want of a better word, fidgety! This form of ADHD is usually noticed in the classroom environment as kids with this type of ADHD find it difficult to concentrate and so can be a little disruptive.

I'm chuckling as I type this because my son's teacher would have disagreed with the 'little' disruptive part. Society has a habit of stereotyping certain 'expected' behaviors. And for the most part, this is a good thing because 'sitting still' is required in specific settings.

Can you imagine how chaotic board meetings and university lectures would be if everyone was running about and not listening? While they'd probably be a lot more fun, unfortunately, it would also mean nothing would get done. However, my point is to remember to smile at your child's exuberance and celebrate them. This is who they are, busy, sometimes inappropriately active, but for the most part, happy, healthy, and yours.

Symptoms:

  ◇ Feel restless and fidget or squirm (taps hands/feet)
  ◇ Talks constantly
  ◇ Cannot sit still for any length of time (work or school)
  ◇ Frequently interrupts conversations (shouts out answers)
  ◇ Struggles to be patient
  ◇ Physically active at inappropriate times (running/climbing)
  ◇ Unable to quietly entertain themselves (reading/puzzles/coloring)
  ◇ Appears constantly busy, unable to slow down

- **Combined presentation**

The combined type of ADHD is when inattentive and hyperactive symptoms are present. However, before you panic, this doesn't automatically mean the Combined presentation type is a more severe form of ADHD! In fact, usually, the symptoms are generally spread evenly between the two types. So, a child presenting with combined ADHD will be both fidgety and inattentive.

This can make for a rather rough combination, leaving you feeling as though you are dealing with ten wild cats on a collision course to nowhere. At least that was my personal experience most school mornings!

SIGNS AND SYMPTOMS OF ADHD

Unfortunately, the signs and symptoms of ADHD can present in many ways, as I am sure you can see from the above lists! Unfortunately, this means it doesn't conform to handy tick list exercises, which would make things a whole lot easier. It's pretty sneaky that way!

Furthermore, in some cases, the above symptoms may indicate other behavioral or medical conditions in children unrelated to ADHD. Therefore, a primary factor when using these symptoms to spot ADHD is identifying if they negatively impact the ability to function effectively both at home and in the school environment.

CAUSES OF ADHD

Before we go one step further, let me clarify that ADHD is not the result of anything you did wrong. So often, parents blame themselves, believing they could have done something to prevent ADHD. But the truth is the real cause of ADHD is unknown. Although much research has gone into this condition, experts are still unsure why it occurs. What they do know is that ADHD is genetic – so if you or your partner have it, the chances you will pass it on to your children are pretty high.

According to some references, it is considered a brain-based biological disorder, which before you panic, simply means it affects the brain chemicals.

Children with ADHD usually have low levels of a particular brain chemical called Dopamine. This chemical has the primary job of being the brain's messenger. However, this is where it gets interesting; it's also directly involved with things like learning, memory, coordination, movement, and activities requiring attention and focus! Woah! I don't know about you, but when I discovered that, suddenly a lot of things made sense!

In addition, brain imaging studies using PET scanners (positron emission tomography) have made it possible to study the brain while working. They have noticed that children with ADHD have a lower brain metabolism in areas of the brain that control movement, attention, and judgment.

DIAGNOSIS OF ADHD

Although ADHD is primarily diagnosed in childhood, there are also instances where a diagnosis is made in adulthood (after age 17). Enter center stage Lina Cole, me, and one charming adult son!

Diagnosis is different for children and adults:

- **Diagnosis in children and teenagers**

Children and teenagers (up to age 16) must display six or more symptoms of ADHD, which need to be present for a minimum of six months. However, the symptom severity should be such that it is considered inappropriate for their age. For example, most five-year-olds fidget a little when sitting for long periods (an appropriate level of development). However, if your teenage child can't sit through their school lessons, that is considered inappropriate for their developmental level.

- **Diagnosis in adults**

Adults aged 17 years and older must display five or more ADHD symptoms. Again, these should be present for a minimum of six months. However, their symptoms might show up slightly differently. For example, an adult struggling with hyperactive-impulsive ADHD may appear extremely restless.

Aside from ADHD symptoms and the number of each required to diagnose it in children or adults, certain conditions need to be met simultaneously. These include:

⋄ Several symptoms were present before age 12
⋄ Symptoms affect multiple settings (home, school, friends, work)
⋄ The symptoms don't relate to another condition (depression, anxiety, or personality disorder)
⋄ Symptoms negatively impact effective functioning at school, work, or socially

WHEN BOTH PARENTS HAVE ADHD

As I mentioned earlier, ADHD is genetic. So, it should come as no surprise that as you travel along the ADHD path with your child, suddenly it looks very familiar! Often one or both parents realize that they also have ADHD when their children are diagnosed with the condition. Aside from the stigma and lack of knowledge surrounding the condition, ADHD was simply not given a second thought by parents in our day. As a result, you were just naughty or lazy!

Thankfully a lot has changed since then, but unfortunately, it does mean that many people are only diagnosed later in life.

Often parents with ADHD find their parenting role overwhelming as they struggle to meet the demands of the kids, home, and work. This is further compounded by the fact that their lack of organizational and disciplinary skills may cause them to struggle to meet their children's needs.

Studies have shown that when caregivers also have ADHD, it can impact the ADHD treatment given to the child. For example, consistency in arranging and managing doctors' appointments, behavioral therapies, medicines, and prescriptions can be challenging.

- **Moms With ADHD**

Discovering you have ADHD as a mother can be particularly distressing. Aren't you supposed to be a perfect, nurturing caregiver? Don't be so hard on yourself! Often, we moms go undiagnosed because, as children, girls with ADHD present differently from boys. Most girls tend to have the inattentive form of ADHD. This means that instead of acting out or being super hyper, they're generally quieter and thus overlooked.

When they eventually seek help, they're more likely to be diagnosed with anxiety or depression rather than ADHD because women are automatically associated with these issues.

Often Moms with ADHD will admit to having found school challenging and organizing their schedules an impossible task. Has much changed now that you are an adult? Probably not, which is why if, as a mother, you are struggling with ADHD, you may find that you often feel very stressed about juggling work, family, house chores, and the kids! You're probably thinking – don't all moms feel this way? Yes, to an extent, but those without ADHD find it easier to prioritize and manage. As a mom with ADHD, you may feel like a failure because although you know what needs doing, actually doing it presents a significant challenge.

- **Who Diagnoses Adult ADHD?**

An adult ADHD diagnosis should be conducted by a licensed physician or mental health professional (self-diagnosis isn't a thing!) Besides, you may learn to 'forgive' yourself a little with an actual diagnosis.

Often parents feel responsible for ADHD, that they have somehow failed as parents, but this isn't true. Perhaps receiving confirmation that you are not a bad parent will help with those feelings of guilt you struggle with each day? The thing to remember is that ADHD is not a failure; it's a genetic disorder.

Professionals who may be able to assist with a diagnosis include your family doctor, psychiatrist, clinical psychologist, clinical social worker, and neurologist.

- **Treating Parents With ADHD**

Stimulants or behavioral therapies can be used to enhance their coping skills as parents. Treatment can also improve parenting skills and reduce the chaos and stress in the home. In some medical settings, professionals will work with both parents and children, discussing their strengths and weaknesses and helping to formulate a cohesive, positive approach to family life.

- **Common Myths About ADHD**

I just love it when people prove their ignorance by jumping on the proverbial bandwagon with these little morsels of misinformation. Of course, if you have a child with ADHD, you know exactly what I mean! So, let's take a quick peek at some of these rumors and NOT proven claims.

◇ **Eating too much sugar causes ADHD**

While excess sugar can make the hyperactive symptoms of ADHD worse, it does not cause ADHD. ADHD is a genetic disorder, not a sugar-related health condition. However, if you consume excessive amounts of sugar, you'll likely struggle with cavities, obesity, and type 2 diabetes. Health lesson over!

◇ **Watching TV & Playing Video games**

There are a lot of theories on this but no evidence to suggest an actual link between ADHD and watching TV or playing video games. In fact, many kids who don't watch TV have also been diagnosed with this condition.

◇ **Poverty**

Many opinions on this one suggest that those from poorer backgrounds are more likely to develop ADHD. Think about this logically, how can being poor affect a genetic condition? It's more likely that if you struggled with ADHD and didn't get the support you needed, you would not be very successful in adult life. Many people with ADHD struggle in the work environment. Therefore, it seems untreated ADHD is more likely to cause poverty, not the other way around!

◇ **Poor parenting**

ADHD is a medical condition that causes behavioral problems. No amount of discipline, as in shouting, rulemaking, or punishment, will change their behavior or the fact that parenting a kid with ADHD is challenging. This genetic condition is not something you did to your child, nor is it the result of poor parenting styles.

Understanding ADHD, its types, and how they present in the 'real' world is essential when raising a child with this condition. I like to call this being 'armed' with the correct knowledge. After all, how can you do battle with the enemy if you don't understand its weaknesses? Not that ADHD is the enemy, but it can be without the proper coping mechanisms. This is why the next part of our journey investigates and addresses the challenges of parenting a child with ADHD. Join me in chapter two as we enter the world of ADHD, aka the war zone!

2

CHALLENGES OF PARENTING AN ADHD KID

"ADHD is just another word for fun, exciting and adventurous."

— JULIE POSEY

My family comes from a close-knit community; everyone knows everyone, and those who don't know you, haven't visited the neighborhood. In our area, people like Mrs. Day peer over the fence for a chat as you root around in your veggie patch, shout at your kids for being too noisy and quietly tell you that you left your garden rake outside last night. Thanks, Mrs. Day; I realized that at 11 pm last night while doing my routine bedside pacing, waiting for Zac to drop off to sleep.

Some nights are better than others when it comes to sleep, but most are fraught with multiple trips to the loo, rechecking his miniature cars are perfectly aligned on the windowsill, and frequent requests for the same story repeatedly ad nauseam. Like most kids with ADHD, Zac finds comfort in repetition. I like to think of it as the glue that anchors him to this world, and without it, he gets very unsettled and anxious. Hence those breakfast cereal battles in those early days!

You may also recognize this poor sleeping pattern as one your kid displays. This is because kids with ADHD can struggle with poor sleep patterns and OCD or other mental health issues due to low dopamine, norepinephrine levels, and high serotonin levels. ADHD often has co-existing or co-occurring conditions – this is where two or more conditions present simultaneously. While ADHD can also co-exist with other issues such as anxiety or depression, it has chosen OCD for my son. Thanks, ADHD; I needed the extra chaos in my already manic household!

This means that it takes an unusually long time for Zac to fall asleep at night and his bedtime routine is super structured. Usually, I wake up to find I've fallen asleep on the floor next to his bed from sheer exhaustion.

Hence my rake-perceiving skills at that late hour! Unfortunately, sleep deprivation and feeling exhausted the next day is part of the drill as the parent of an ADHD kid.

Cue the copious amounts of coffee we drink daily to keep us marginally functioning. My local Starbucks knows me by name and, most mornings has my order ready to go as I walk in the door! Anyway, my point is that Mrs. Day and others frequently feel the need to offer useless advice, usually at points when biting my tongue requires Olympic skill.

Not to mention the hurtful comments that others feel they need to throw into the mix. No, I'm not a bad parent, I'm not just giving in to his tantrums, nor am I facilitating his bad behavior by not reacting in what society feels is an 'appropriate' parental manner.

What I am is a tired parent with a child who has a chronic disorder that requires ongoing management and support. Unfortunately, no amount of discipline or supposed 'strictness' is going to resolve the genuine presence of ADHD that my son struggles with each day.

If only I had been braver in those days, I probably would have spent far less time worrying about Zac's behavior and more time enjoying his childhood. And possibly more time in the garden instead of playing 'comment-dodge-ball' with Mrs. Day.

The fact is, parenting a kid with ADHD presents some very real challenges for both the child and the parent/s, many of which the average person doesn't understand and can't even begin to imagine. As a result, after a plethora of misguided advice and hurtful judgments, we parents learn to keep silent and stop trying to explain the situation, thus creating our own ADHD prison of existence.

Take a look at the below rather shocking facts I've come across in my search to tame the dragon that is ADHD:

- According to a 2008 study, 23% of married couples who had kids diagnosed with ADHD were divorced.
- Raising kids with ADHD is getting more difficult by the day, as parents endure several challenges and get minimum to no support from families or friends.

PARENTAL CHALLENGES

After an ADHD diagnosis, it can seem like a whirlwind has ripped your life apart. It has, but things will settle; trust me, I'm a whirlwind survivor! However, many parents only cope- marginally and sadly often without the support of family or friends.

- **Marital stress**

The study I mentioned earlier found that parents of ADHD children are more likely to divorce than those with kids who didn't have the condition. Let's be frank here, marriage comes with its own stress levels (chore wars and shopping list debates) and adding ADHD can sometimes be like adding Tic Tacs to cola – explosive!

The frustrations of parenting kids with ADHD can cause a lot of tension between couples. Now add that many of these parents have limited alone time, coupled with a dash of sleep deprivation, and you have the reason why divorce may feel like it's the only solution.

Instead, try to spend time alone together regularly and discuss the issues your child is struggling with calmly and respectfully.

- **Isolation**

Parents with ADHD kids often feel like they are isolated in their situation. After all, everyone else's kids around them seem perfect and trouble-free. However, there are many in the same situation as you; it's simply a case of knowing where to find like-minded friends.

Joining an online or face-to-face support group can link you to other parents traveling the same path as you. An excellent example of online support and resources is CHADD (Children and Adults with Attention Deficit/Hyperactivity Disorder).

- **Boredom**

Kids with ADHD get bored very quickly, but this doesn't mean you don't get bored yourself! Be honest with yourself; it can be very tedious and extremely exhausting saying the same things repeatedly.

Instead, take a walk or sit outside in the sun while savoring a well-deserved coffee or tea break. Self-care is essential; if you don't provide proper care for yourself, how will you care for your child?

- **Feelings of guilt**

We all struggle with feelings of guilt, but ADHD seems to place them under the microscope. Perhaps you feel responsible for your child's ADHD, or maybe you're so tired you lose your patience at times; this is normal. Even if you find yourself screeching from the top of the stairs, hair on end with one stock on and your bra on backward!

Just because your child has ADHD hasn't turned you into Superman capable of doing everything perfectly and at speed. Although, at times, wearing your underpants on top of your clothes may seem like the best look to rock this week! Instead, tap into your sense of humor and realize that feelings of guilt are normal for parents raising kids with learning differences. Accept it. Move on.

- **Burden of care**

The burden of care can feel insurmountable, especially if you are a single parent or the primary caregiver. This added to financial worries can impact your quality of life and mental health. According to a 2005 study, ADHD places a significant financial burden on families.

"Results of the medical cost studies consistently indicated that children with ADHD had higher annual medical costs than either matched control."

Depending on where you live, you may be able to ask for financial aid from government-based programs administered by your local Social Security Administration office.

- **Stigmatization**

Our own self-stigmatization tells us we are poor parents because our kids are struggling. The first step to eliminating this stigma, self-proclaimed or otherwise, is recognizing it as a legitimate disorder. Rather than hiding it or pretending it doesn't exist, stare it in the eye. Accept the reality of ADHD, and then seek out the help and support you need to defeat it!

- **Struggle to keep up with routines of everyday life**

ADHD is like a rubber ball, it doesn't fit into schedules easily, and frequently ping pongs off the proverbial walls of life. No matter how structured your routines might be, ADHD has a habit of stepping in and causing chaos at a moment's notice.

On top of providing the needed support to your child, you still need to fulfill the essential functions of everyday living. Suddenly, washing, cleaning, dog walking, and cooking a balanced meal can seem like uphill challenges.

Children with ADHD benefit from completing chores around the home. It can help them feel they provide a positive contribution to family life. So, my advice is to get them helping not only does it help them, it helps you too.

KIDS AND BAD BEHAVIOR

- **Why kids with ADHD act out**

The hyperactive and super impulsive symptoms of ADHD can make sitting still or staying in a specific area seem very restrictive to kids desperate to explore and discover what lies beyond the park's boundaries or behind a closed department store door. This impulsive behavior leads to stressed parenting styles such as yelling, hanging onto little hands, etc.

This doesn't make you a bad parent, on the contrary, you don't want your kid to be run over by a car or lost in the shops, so it makes sense. However, this negative interaction between parent and child causes aggression or acting out. If you are constantly told you are wrong, you start to either believe it or react negatively in rebellion.

- **Why do they throw tantrums?**

Tasks that require a lot of effort or are repetitive can be challenging for kids with ADHD. For example, homework, bedtime, or getting dressed can literally start World War Three. Typically, children with ADHD use tantrums, power struggles, and even blatant defiance as their avoidance weapon of choice.

As a result, you may change the task which provides the solution they wanted. However, if you don't yield and resort to punishments and yelling, it results in further negative interaction- enter the proverbial vicious circle. Unfortunately, this doesn't work; being constantly in trouble simply desensitizes them to the situation, and eventually, they don't care about punishments one way or the other.

- **How ADHD and bad behavior aren't the same**

People often think that ADHD and bad behavior are synonymous. They are not. ADHD is a neurological and genetic disorder that imbalances the brain. Hyperactive and inattentive symptoms associated with ADHD can make certain repetitive or effort-requiring tasks formidable to kids with ADHD. As a result, shouting, pushing, or throwing things are their only way of communicating this stress as they struggle to manage their feelings.

IS IT REALLY ADHD?

ADHD has many symptoms that mimic those of other conditions. In addition, children with ADHD are more at risk of other mental health issues such as anxiety and depression. This co-existence of conditions is why the root cause of ADHD is often missed.

▷ **Bipolar disorder**

Characteristics: Severe changes in mood, behavior, energy, and thinking

Similarities: mood changes, impatience, outbursts, hyperactivity, incessant talking

Why it's not ADHD: Bipolar disorder primarily affects a person's mood.

▷ **Autism**

Characteristics: Appear detached from surroundings, struggle socially, emotional immaturity.

Similarities: hyperactivity, impaired social development, lack of focus, learning difficulties

Why it's not ADHD: Autism affects speech development, communication, and social interaction. It also includes repetitive behaviors like pacing or rocking sensory issues like being under or reactive to touch, taste, smell, or light.

▷ **Low Blood Sugar Level**

Characteristics: Aggression, difficulty concentrating, hyperactivity, fidgety

Similarities: hyperactivity, aggression, inattentiveness

Why it's not ADHD: When sugar levels return to normal, the symptoms disappear.

▷ **Sensory Processing Disorder**

Characteristics: Under or over sensitivity to sensory factors such as smell, sight, taste, touch, smell, or movement.

Similarities: Inability to concentrate, hyperactivity, difficulty concentrating

Why it's not ADHD: Overstimulation is regulated by removing sensory input triggers.

▷ **Sleep disorder**

Characteristics: Difficulty concentrating and following instructions, affects short-term memory, inattentiveness.

Similarities: Inattentiveness, struggles to follow directions, forgetful

Why it's not ADHD: Once the sleep disorder is addressed, for example, sleep apnea, RLS (restless legs syndrome), or night terrors, the symptoms improve.

▷ **Hearing problems**

Characteristics: Inattentiveness, struggle to concentrate, easily distracted, lack of focus, poor communication skills.

Similarities: Lack of focus, poor social skills, struggles to communicate

Why it's not ADHD: Symptoms improve once the hearing problem is identified, and the necessary support is provided.

▷ **Kids being kids**

Characteristics: Easily bored, excitable, immature, or overly mature

Similarities: Boredom, easily distracted, inattentive or hyperactive

Why it's not ADHD: Kids, in general, are bouncy, fun-loving creatures that are easily excited or bored. Misdiagnosis can occur when younger children are stereotyped by teachers/parents who believe an excitable child is emotionally immature compared to their peers. Alternatively, intelligent kids might become quickly bored if the work/task doesn't present enough of a challenge.

COPING WITH ADHD STIGMA

According to some paraphrased definitions, a stigma is a substantial lack of respect for someone because they have either done something or are something SOCIETY disapproves of. It seems a little unfair that ADHD has an attached stigma seeing as those who have it didn't choose it or do anything to get it!

Why Does ADHD Carry A Stigma?

Unfortunately, although there is a lot of evidence to support the fact that ADHD is a genuine medical condition, many people still don't recognize it as such. Instead, it's a common misconception that ADHD is an excuse for laziness or sloppiness. As a result, many people also believe that taking medication or receiving behavioral treatment for ADHD is overrated and a further justification for poor performance in everyday life.

What Are The Popular Stigmas On ADHD?

- ADHD isn't real
- Parents need to push harder
- Medication is an easy way out

- Kids with ADHD need better parenting

What Harm Does The Stigma Cause?

The stigma of ADHD infiltrates many aspects of a person's life, from school to work and social interactions. Unfortunately, the challenges of this stigma may cause people to avoid getting the help they need. As a direct result, they often suffer from depression, anxiety, poor self-esteem, and poor social interactions. Further issues include relationship problems and parent-child conflict.

Who Is Affected By The Stigma?

Stigmatization is tough for everyone with ADHD. However, it seems girls have it the hardest. ADHD is often thought of as a male problem. As a result, girls struggling with ADHD are often stereotyped as having 'something wrong.' In addition, ADHD is also thought to be a childhood disease. Therefore, adults who have the condition are viewed negatively as others believe they are using it to excuse their lack of achievement in life.

Coping With Hurtful Comments

Nowadays, when people start their sentences with things like; 'In my day,' 'When I was a kid,' or my personal favorite, 'May I offer you some advice'– I smile and mentally wave bye-bye.

That's not to say I don't care what others say, nor do I feel I know everything; it's simply my coping mechanism and prevents me from getting hurt and feeling undermined.

Unfortunately, people will have opinions, but that's all they are -opinions. According to some broad definitions I've seen floating around the internet, an opinion is a judgment or view not based on FACT or KNOWLEDGE. So I say, toss them out the proverbial window; something that isn't true or backed by fact isn't worth much anyway.

Counteracting The Effects Of ADHD Stereotyping

Nothing feels better than taking positive action in the face of adversity. Get involved with educating others and yourself about this condition, its effects, and its reality. Knowledge is definitely power when faced with ADHD. Stand up for fellow ADHD survivors and get involved with local charitable ADHD organizations. The more awareness we as parents generate, the less stereotyping there will be!

Parental Advice On ADHD Stigmatization

While your child needs to understand their diagnosis, ensure they recognize that it's not an excuse for poor behavior but the reason for the challenges they face. Also, ensure your child has the support they need at school and in other settings, many of which are obligated to accommodate their unique learning needs.

While ADHD is a battle involving seemingly insurmountable parental challenges, diagnosis, and unfair stigmatization, it's not the final battle. And if you learn that not every skirmish requires full-combat gear, the fight becomes less of a war and more of a compromised and calm co-existence.

3
EXECUTIVE FUNCTION 101

"People who have never dealt with mental illness will never understand, know how legitimately triumphant it feels to decide to take a shower and then actually do it."

— RUBY WALKER

Executive function is our brain's ability to control the many areas in our lives that require self-control. This plays out in daily life, affecting our motivation to start or complete tasks, attentiveness, planning, organizing, and concentration.

When this function is impaired, it's called executive *dysfunction*, and for good reasons, because it affects a person's ability to start and complete a task from start to finish. As parents of ADHD children, you know more than most how frustrating it is to watch your child start a task, get distracted, and wander off to something entirely different. Hence, the homework battles, toothpaste wars, bathtime skirmishes, and plethora of lost or misplaced items of clothing, keys, toys, etc.

Interestingly enough, EF symptoms don't only affect those with ADHD; they can also affect those who have autism, depression, and other learning or mental health disorders.

According to well-known ADHD therapist Billy Roberts, LISW-S founder and owner of Focused Mind ADHD, "If someone has ADHD, they have executive dysfunction. However, if someone has executive dysfunction, that doesn't mean they have ADHD." This is because EF can be caused by various cognitive function issues, including ADHD, depression, and other learning disorders.

In other words, EF is not a disorder but rather a set of symptoms linked to conditions that affect the brain's ability to effectively manage certain skill sets such as memory, planning, attention, time management, and organizational skills.

These are skills that most people depend on without even realizing; however, for those with ADHD and other conditions, they may seem virtually impossible. In addition, other areas that executive function effects are behavior and emotion control, multitasking, and problem-solving.

Is your child's behavior suddenly making sense? For me, understanding EF was my first light bulb moment. Now I understood why my son seemed so scatter-brained and emotionally out of control.

SIGNS OF EXECUTIVE DYSFUNCTION

Executive dysfunction affects multiple areas of a person's life. Unlike someone who is sometimes late for work or occasionally forgets where they have put their keys, executive dysfunction negatively impacts a person's life in more than one area daily.

- Misses' deadlines
- Always late to school, work, or social activities
- Struggles to pay attention
- Forgetfulness
- Emotional outbursts
- Frequently loses or misplaces things

These symptoms can cause chaos in busy family life and place a lot of pressure on your child. Can you imagine being in trouble all the time for things you simply can't control or seem to manage?

STRESS AND EXECUTIVE FUNCTION

As a rule, stress isn't great for anyone; now, add the complexities of ADHD and the symptoms of executive function to the mix, and you have a recipe for disaster.

When stressed, the adrenal gland automatically secretes high cortisol levels (stress hormone), which affects the functioning of the brain's prefrontal cortex or, as I like to call them, executive- function headquarters. Of course, this happens to all humans, but when executive functions are already impaired, as in the case of ADHD, can you imagine the issues it will cause?

STRESS VS. EXECUTIVE FUNCTION

The scary reality is that stress can increase ADHD symptoms and affect how your child develops and learns. Even worse, kids with ADHD struggle with stress more than those without this chronic condition. So how do we mitigate the effects of stress? First, let's look at the areas it affects.

1. Working memory (short-term memory)

Enables us to retain information required to complete tasks such as reading, learning, reasoning, and language comprehension. Stress impacts the ability to create short-term memories and turn them into long-term ones, making learning difficult.

2. Inhibition (automatic or impulsive responses)

This is our ability to focus/ignore distractions and control our reactions or responses (verbal or physical) to outside stimuli or internal frustrations. For example, choosing not to throw a tantrum, scream, or lash out when angry. ADHD and stress are the perfect combos for the emotional roller coaster you, as ADHD parents witness regularly.

3. Cognitive flexibility

This is our ability to multitask, problem-solve, switch between tasks and adapt to changing situations. In other words, the ability to recognize, adapt to and tolerate unexpected changes. For example, you realize you've run out of bread and can't make your lunch. Do you get angry and refuse to eat anything or select something else to eat? Do you go to the café and eat there?

Cognitive flexibility is the ability to consider other options if things change unexpectedly. This would explain those cereal wars in my house. If we ran out, my son's poor cognitive flexibility wouldn't allow him to recognize the other options he could select. This resulted in terrible tantrums, and as a result, I'm embarrassed to say I found myself stockpiling the darn stuff to ensure we had enough to feed an army!

STRATEGIES TO REDUCE STRESS WITH ADHD

ADHD creates a lot of stress in an individual's life. This has a knock-on effect causing ADHD symptoms to increase, increasing the pressure on executive functions, and negatively impacting daily life. Learning how to reduce stress is the key to soothing the symptoms of executive dysfunction and calming the ADHD storm. This can be done in several ways:

- Psychotherapy or coaching

This can help identify stress <u>triggers</u> and develop ways to manage them in daily life.

- Adopt A Healthy lifestyle

A daily routine, healthy diet, sufficient sleep, and regular exercise are the primary ingredients for reducing stress.

- Embrace Proper Sleep Patterns

Create a proper sleep routine involving regular bedtime and waking at the same time each morning. Avoid overstimulation caused by technology (TV, PC games) before bedtime.

- Exercise Regularly

Regular exercise is a natural mood enhancer that boosts feel-good endorphins and helps control ADHD symptoms.

Go For A Walk In Nature

According to a national study conducted by Frances E. Kuo, natural green spaces could be a potential natural treatment for ADHD.

"Green outdoor settings appear to reduce ADHD symptoms in children across a wide range of individual, residential, and case characteristics."

- Practice Breathing exercises

Recognize when you feel stressed, then take a moment to sit in a quiet place. Close your eyes and take 10 slow, measured breaths. Then go for a brief 5-minute walk outside

- Start Journaling

Make it part of your daily routine to write down your thoughts, emotions, and worries. This process can help you slow down, focus on your thoughts, and problem solve. In addition, the simple act of writing down your feelings can alleviate the stress you are experiencing.

EXECUTIVE FUNCTION AND BRAIN DEVELOPMENT

According to a study released in 2017 and published by The Lancet of Psychiatry, children with ADHD have 5 out of 7 brain regions smaller than kids without ADHD. The Amygdala, responsible for self-control and emotional control, showed the most significant size difference.

This size difference seems to even out in the teenage years, but that doesn't mean that ADHD symptoms magically disappear. ADHD is a lifelong brain disorder. However, there are treatments, therapies, and coping strategies that will ensure they live well-rounded and adjusted lives!

The reason I mentioned this study is to show you that the brains of children with ADHD develop at a slower rate, FACT. Furthermore, it's an actual condition, not a made-up excuse for badly behaved children!

This means that certain self-management areas of the brain take a little longer to develop with ADHD. These include:

Brain Area	Regulates
Caudate Nucleus	Decision making, purposed behavior
Putamen	Learning, memory, movement
Cerebral Cortex	Self-management
Nucleus Accumbens	Mood, pleasure, motivation
Amygdala	Prioritizing actions, emotional control
Hippocampus	Short & long term memory

For the brain to function seamlessly, these brain areas need to work together like well-oiled cogs. To do this, the brain cells pass information from one neuron to the next by releasing chemicals called neurotransmitters which bridge the gap between the neurons. However, add ADHD to the mix, and suddenly this process is a lot more choppy and disconnected. This can affect the process in several ways, resulting in many of the challenges associated with ADHD.

- Sending neuron releases too little chemical (neurotransmitter)
- Receiving neuron misses the neurotransmitter
- Sending neuron snatches the neurotransmitter back before it reaches the receiving neuron.

STRATEGIES TO IMPROVE EXECUTIVE FUNCTION

If your child has ADHD, they will definitely struggle with executive dysfunction. Unfortunately, these two are firm friends in the world of ADHD! However, before you admit defeat (we ADHD parents never give up!), let's review the three core executive functions and some nifty coping strategies you can employ in everyday life.

3 Core Executive Functions

#1 Inhibitory Control

▷ **Behavior**

The key element here is self-control. For example, resisting impulse or temptation and thinking before speaking or taking action. These tie into self-discipline, remaining focused even when bored or getting the task wrong.

Activity/Strategy

- Drama – acting out a character
- Co Reading – taking turns to be the reader/listener
- Games like Simple Simon Says and Do This, Do That

▷ **Attention**

This is the ability to remain focused and ignore distractions even when bored.

Activity/Strategy

- Listening to stories read aloud, but without visual aids such as pictures or puppets. This means the listener needs to work harder on remaining focused.
- Singing in a round, where each singer sings the same words and melody but begins and ends at different times.
- Walking while balancing on a log or tires in the playground.

#2 **Working Memory**

This is the ability to use short-term memory to complete tasks, follow instructions and remember questions.

Activity/Strategy

- Mental math, adding up the shopping list as you go around the supermarket.
- Storytelling/listening to stories
- Following a simple list of chores (sweep the floor, pick up the toys)

#3 **Cognitive Flexibility**

This is the ability to multitask, problem-solve, switch between tasks and adapt to changing situations.

Activity/Strategy

- Problem-solving games such as Hide & Seek & Hunt The Thimble
- Activities requiring improvisation such as expressive dance, theater, and playing jazz.

AGE-APPROPRIATE ACTIVITIES TO IMPROVE EXECUTIVE FUNCTION IN KIDS

To kick start executive function into action, kids need to learn how to flex their EF muscles. Games can be used to practice executive function skills that require memory, attention, and self-control. The trick is not to choose games that are too challenging at first; once they are familiar with the game, move on to something a little more challenging.

For 5-7-year-olds

▷ **Card & Board Games**

Memory Games – **Concentration, Go Fish, Old Maid.**

Remembering the location of specific cards is excellent for flexing the working memory muscle.

Matching Games – **Uno, Crazy Eights**

Playing card games by suit or numbers strengthen cognitive flexibility.

Attention & Inhibition – **Snap**

Fast-moving games like snap challenge attention and inhibition processes.

▷ **Physical Activities/Games**

Attention – Musical Chairs, Red light, Green Light

Games that require a fast response or action help children practice attention and inhibition skills. They also help with improving working memory as the children monitor the movements of the other players.

Decision Making & Self-Control – Dodge ball, Tetherball

These types of games require the players to pay attention, follow the rules and make quick decisions such as jumping or moving out of the way of the ball.

Cognitive Flexibility – Hide & Seek, Simon Says

Games, where the rules and subsequent actions change quickly, are excellent for strengthening cognitive flexibility, attention, and inhibition.

▷ **Movement/Song Games**

Working Memory & Inhibition – Down Down Baby, Miss Mary Mack

Clapping rhythms that follow a repetitive pattern enable your child to practice working memory, cognitive flexibility, and inhibition skills.

Working Memory – We're going on a bear hunt, Packing for a Picnic

Repetitive songs that require additional information to be added to each verse as the song progresses are a super way to challenge working memory.

▷ **Quiet Activities Requiring Strategies and Reflection/Brain Teasers**

Selective Attention – I Spy

Games like 'I Spy' challenge children to use selective attention skills when searching for the correct item or object. It also helps with inhibition as they practice self-control, waiting for their turn, and cognitive flexibility in following rules.

Working Memory & Flexible Thinking – Brain teasers, Mazes, Word Matching

Puzzles, brain teasers, and word or picture matching games ideally exercise working memory and cognitive flexibility.

For 7-12-year-olds

▷ **Card and Board Games**

Working Memory & Mental Flexibility – Hearts, Bridge, Rummy

Playing cards requires strategy, planning, and in some cases, matching. This provides a workout for working memory and enhances mental flexibility.

Attention & Decision Making – Chess, Go, Dungeons & Dragons, Minecraft

Planning and strategizing are required when playing these games. They're great for stimulating working memory and cognitive flexibility as players need to follow the rules and adjust their moves to reach the desired income.

▷ **Physical Activities/Games**

Cognitive Flexibility, Working Memory & Attention – All Forms of Sports

Sports such as soccer, basketball, and hockey, are excellent for improving all executive functions. Activities like these that require coordination, following rules, and strategizing can improve the core functions of executive control.

Attention & Working Memory – Jump Rope, Chinese Jump Rope

Jump rope games require focused practice, attention, and drawing on working memory. This means players need to focus and remain attentive while jumping the rope and recalling the words to the song.

▷ **Movement/Song Games**

Working Memory & Self-Monitoring – Learning to Play a Musical Instrument

Learning to play musical instruments such as the piano or drums simultaneously challenges selective attention and self-monitoring. It also stimulates working memory as the learner needs to hold the music in mind while playing and following the rhythm.

Cognitive Flexibility, Memory, Attention – Singing In Rounds

Singing in a group challenge working memory, self-monitoring, and selective attention.

Working Memory, Attention, Self-Monitoring – Dance

Learning to follow a specific set of dance moves to music requires drawing on working memory, attention, and self-monitoring. Dancers need to remain focused on the rhythm and pattern of the music and exercise working memory to coordinate their movements.

▷ Quiet Activities Requiring Strategies and Reflection/Brain Teasers

Working Memory – Puzzles, Rubik's Cube, Crossword Puzzles

Puzzles require information to be held and used in working memory to find their potential solution. They are the perfect challenge for stimulating the core executive functions, working memory, cognitive flexibility, and inhibition.

For Infants

Using different activities to develop executive functions from an early age is highly beneficial for your child's development, whether they have ADHD or not. From the moment they are born, children are like little sponges, absorbing and learning from their surrounding environment.

Most of the below activities are traditionally used to entertain kids, but did you realize the significant impact they have on attentiveness, concentration, and working memory?

▷ **Lap Games With Hand Clapping**

Concentration, Working Memory & Impulse Control

Lap games usually involve rhythmic clapping along to a song or chant. In the beginning, you set the pace and rhythm as they learn to remain concentrated on what you are doing. Then, as their working memory and concentration skills develop, they will start to join in and coordinate their clapping.

▷ **Peek-a-boo**

Working Memory

Peek-a-boo is an excellent game for developing working memory. The game's primary purpose is for them to remember who is hiding while remaining focused on the game. In the beginning, they may lose concentration and cry or get distracted if you take too long to reappear.

However, as their ability to hold both you and the game in their working memory develops, they will learn to wait for you to reappear or start looking for you. This game also enhances cognitive flexibility and develops the ability to control emotions and reactions to changing situations.

▷ Hiding Toys/Objects

Working Memory & Speech Development

Hiding toys or objects for your child to find is an excellent way to enhance working memory, improve their attention span and develop self-control. Start by hiding them in easy-to-find places behind your back or under a cloth or blanket. Then, during the game, chat about where the item could be, ask questions, and state when the item is found. Even if you don't get a response, this verbal engagement encourages speech development.

▷ Singing Along With Fingerplay

Speech Development, Concentration, Working Memory & Self-Regulation

Songs that require fingerplays, such as Itsy Bitsy Spider, This Little Piggy Went To Market, and Two Little Dickie Birds Sitting On A Wall, are perfect for developing working memory, concentration, and speech. At first, you will need to help them imitate the actions, but they will start doing this for themselves as they develop.

▷ **Copycat**

Self-Regulation, Concentration, Working Memory & Coordination

Copycat games where your child learns to copy your actions are perfect developmental tools for several reasons. First, they introduce your child to the concept of interacting with others and waiting their turn (self-regulation). Next, they enhance concentration and focus as they need to remember what your actions were to copy them. Lastly, their reaction to your actions requires coordinated movement.

Copycat games could include copying daily chores (switch off the lights, wipe down the kitchen counter, pick up the toys) or imitating the movements of animals (hop like a bunny, leap like a frog, growl like a bear) and actions songs such as Simple Simon Says.

▷ **Sensory activities**

Speech and Sensory Development

Early years development involves a lot of non-verbal learning as your child's speech develops. Introduce color, texture, and shapes to encourage your child's interest in their surrounding environment. Enhance this developmental tool by attaching words to each sensory experience. For example, if they touch something soft, tell them it feels soft. Learning the meaning of new words with the help of sensory experience makes the learning process much more straightforward!

None of us are born with executive control skills; these develop as we mature. However, in the case of kids with ADHD, they take a little longer to develop. As parents, we can help our kids hone their EF muscles by establishing regular routines and using games to encourage self-control, rule-following, and imagination.

Improving executive function is one of the fundamental keys to calming the storm of ADHD. Strong executive function skills enhance their ability to control, hold, and utilize the information received from their surrounding environment.

Life becomes more manageable, and stress is reduced as they develop healthy habits and routines. As a result, their actions and reactions are more appropriate to changing situations as they learn to navigate the realms of self-control and cognitive flexibility.

4

ADHD AND ADOLESCENCE

"Young people willing to push super hard to make something happen are among the most powerful forces in the world."

— SAM ALTMAN

Throughout my son's junior school years, I lived in perpetual hope that his behavior would improve. Somehow, these tantrums, explosive outbursts, and struggles with schoolwork would magically disappear. Perhaps they were just a phase, something he would grow out of eventually? That was until the reality of teen ADHD exploded into my world with full force!

The fact is, ADHD is a neurodevelopmental disorder, and it's not something that disappears overnight. While the average age of diagnosis is 7-years old, ADHD symptoms continue to make their presence known well into adolescence and adulthood. The truth is those tantrums don't go away; they just get bigger! Let me explain a little further.

We all know that adolescence is a particularly stressful time in life. Teens struggle with so much change, physically, mentally, and emotionally that the negative impact of these stresses can often result in depression, anxiety, inappropriate behaviors, substance abuse, and even suicide.

Now add ADHD to this shopping list of worrying teenage issues, and you have the perfect recipe for a Molotov cocktail! Unfortunately, unlike those tasty holiday drinks found on sandy beach holidays, this cocktail is true to its definition and is one that's bound to explode!

That said, there are ways to manage Teen ADHD effectively and positively, thus encouraging your teen to live a well-balanced and productive life while dealing with the stresses of adolescence. We as parents just need to know what to look for and how to deal with it.

I like to think of our parental role as a bit like baseball. As parents, we are the batters facing the opposing pitcher (ADHD); it's our job to bat whatever balls ADHD throws at our teens and help them get to home base (navigate adolescence). But to do this, we need to understand how ADHD presents in teens and the strategies we can use to develop and encourage them during this challenging part of their lives.

The symptoms of ADHD in teens look very similar to those seen in younger children. However, hormonal changes and the increased pressure and responsibility of senior school and extracurricular activities can worsen ADHD symptoms. Furthermore, coping strategies and parental tactics that worked when they were younger may not work now that they are older.

ADHD SYMPTOMS IN TEENS.

- Distracted – starts tasks/projects but struggles to complete them.
- Impulsive – doesn't think things through, makes poor or potentially dangerous decisions.
- Hyperactive – high energy, inability to sit still, always on the go.

- Poor Concentration – struggles to pay attention and follow conversations or instructions.
- Disorganized – poor time management skills, misplaces possessions frequently.

Other symptoms include heightened emotional responses, procrastination, personal hygiene issues, fidgeting, and self-focused tendencies. So how does this affect everyday life? Exponentially!

A teen struggling with ADHD will typically find school life extremely challenging due to their inability to remain focused and concentrate in class. Some teens might find it difficult to sit still in class, maintain attention or interact appropriately during lessons, resulting in frequent interruptions. In addition, forgetting to hand in assignments and struggling to keep track of textbooks or notes is not uncommon for the ADHD teen.

A lack of focus is enemy number one for ADHD teens. Their struggle to complete tasks and their rushed approach to assignments frequently result in mistakes, poor grades, and strained social interactions.

Teens with ADHD struggle to read social cues, not realizing they have offended or upset others. As a result, they are not very adept at compromising, making it tricky to make friends or maintain friendships.

Sadly, this vortex of seemingly constant failure in school and socially is the reason why many teens with ADHD feel demoralized and isolated.

TEEN GENDER & ADHD

While millions of American children have been diagnosed with ADHD, boys are more likely to be diagnosed than girls. According to a 2016 national survey based on children aged 2-17 years, the number of boys diagnosed with ADHD was calculated at 12.9%; this outstripped the number of girls diagnosed, which tallied at a mere 5.6%.

I'm guessing your immediate thought is that girls are less likely to get ADHD? Unfortunately, girls are not immune to ADHD. However, their symptoms present differently and are often overlooked, resulting in a lack of diagnosis.

Unlike the hyperactive symptoms of ADHD seen in boys, such as running around and physical aggression, girls tend to struggle more with inattentive symptoms and are typically more verbally aggressive. This means they are often quieter than their boisterous male counterparts and have fewer behavioral problems. Therefore, a chatty, absent-minded girl doesn't automatically trigger any ADHD warning signs. Unfortunately, the lack of obvious ADHD symptoms also means they aren't referred for diagnosis or treatment.

Girls also tend to hide their symptoms. Blame society, peer pressure, or even cultural inferences; for whatever reason, there is a certain level of expectation when it comes to girls (women in general). They are expected to be organized, tidy, do their homework, and be well-mannered and well-behaved. The teen-girl struggling with ADHD feels this pressure and quickly learns to hide or mask her symptoms. Tactics such as arriving hours early for appointments or class to avoid being late and obsessively checking and rechecking her schedule might be masking techniques, she employs to hide her ADHD without even realizing it.

The effects of upholding this false perfection take their toll on girls' mental and emotional health. Consequently, this has a knock-on effect on their social and academic lives and often results in a diagnosis of mood disorders such as anxiety and depression.

COMMON CHALLENGES OF TEENS WITH ADHD

Risky Behaviors

Climbing mountains, sky-diving, bungee jumping, and driving at extreme speed all have one thing in common; they increase Dopamine levels in the brain. This brain chemical is responsible for providing us with intense feelings of pleasure when doing things that make us feel good.

Things like sex, gambling, drinking alcohol, binge eating, and shopping can all trigger a super Dopamine rush. It's the brain's feel-good reward system, and often it has us eating more pizza than we planned or guzzling down extra choccies when no one is looking. This buzz-inducing chemical is so good at its job that research has linked it to things like drug addiction, alcohol abuse, smoking, and dangerous behaviors.

Now add ADHD to this list of dark issues, and what do we get? Instead of overindulging in a bit of pizza or perhaps occasionally going on an expensive shopping spree, you now have a speed-loving junkie looking for their next Dopamine fix at every opportunity!

But before you start to panic, let's look at why this happens, and then I'll share some helpful tips to help you navigate this bumpy section of the road!

Why does having ADHD increase risky behavior? The answer is quite simple and is the same reason why your child, when they were younger, may have jumped on and off furniture, ran into the road, and disappeared at the park or mall - Dopamine levels.

Those with ADHD typically have lower levels of this feel-good brain chemical. However, when they take risks, it gives them a little boost which they may begin to crave, and as a result, risky behavioral patterns increase.

Typical arguments parents have with their ADHD teens include:

- Driving too fast
- Risky sexual behavior
- Starting fights/arguing
- Underage drinking
- Not taking responsibility for commitments/appointments

That's not to say that all teens with ADHD are going to develop into drug-taking, promiscuous, chocolate hoarders, but it does mean they are at an increased risk of seeking immediate gratification without thought of the consequences.

Lastly, although teenagers all struggle with mood swings and feelings of inadequacy at times, additional factors such as ADHD can magnify these issues. Struggling to fit in socially, peer pressures, and bullying can also contribute to suicidal thoughts and self-harm.

DIAGNOSING ADHD IN TEENS

It can be quite challenging to get an ADHD diagnosis after age 12 as the symptoms need to have been present before this age to qualify. Also, many of the tests for ADHD are focused on the younger child and are not relevant to teens. A teen ADHD assessment should be carried out by a clinician with expertise in ADHD, for example, a psychologist or psychiatrist who specializes in the condition.

Co-Occurring Conditions

Many teens with ADHD also struggle with co-occurring conditions. While these may have been present during childhood, sometimes the stress of adolescence unveils them further! This can make parenting more challenging and, in most cases, find us hiding under the kitchen sink! Unfortunately, co-occurring conditions definitely make parenting harder, especially as more than 60% of teens with ADHD have at least one extra disorder. Thanks, ADHD; you're definitely the gift that doesn't stop giving!

Typical co-occurring conditions seen with ADHD include:

- Oppositional Defiant Disorder (ODD)

Outbursts, irritability, and non-compliance with rules or expectations.

- Conduct Disorder (CD)

Disregards rules, tendency to harm others or animals, steal, trespass, or skip school.

- Depression/Dysthymia

Mood disorders like depression or dysthymia (negative mood)

- Anxiety Disorders

Anxiety attacks and excessive worrying. Physical symptoms may include stomach upsets, headaches, and increased heart rate.

- Learning/communication issues

A decline in academic performance and communication issues such as stuttering, understanding language, or struggling to express themselves.

- Sleep Disturbance

Sleep patterns may change as adolescents stay up later or sleep in later.

PARENTING STRATEGIES FOR TEENS WITH ADHD

Struggling with an obstinate teen is the hardest job parents face in life. However, struggling with a teen that has ADHD requires patience, structure, and a little insanity! Learn to laugh at yourself and the situation and remember what I said about full combat gear; it's not always needed. Now is the time when you learn when to put it on and when to leave it in the wardrobe for another day. Besides, not every day has to be a warzone; sometimes, a little cease-fire is beneficial for both sides!

Behavior Management

- **Involve Teens In Family Rules**

A home without rules is chaos, but a home with enforced rules is worse, especially if your child is struggling with ODD or CD. Instead, encourage input from your teen regarding the rules you have in the home, as this will help them recognize what is expected of them and encourage them to take responsibility.

- **Praise Positive Behaviour**

Everyone enjoys praise; it encourages us to do better and repeat good behavior. Instead of stressing over what they did wrong, praise them for the things they do right and the positive choices they make.

- **Set Consequences**

Discuss appropriate consequences for challenging or difficult behavior with your child. For example, you could agree they lose access to their phone or tv for a certain period if they are aggressive or rude. Consistency is important.

- **Create Daily routines**

Set times for homework, bedtime, chores, and shower time, as this predictable structure will make it easier for them to comply.

- **Driving**

Discuss the responsibility of driving, for example, wearing a seatbelt, sticking to the speed limit, and obeying the rules of the road. Unfortunately, inattention and a lack of inhibition caused by ADHD can make driving challenging resulting in tickets and accidents. Agree on rules that state no phone or eating while driving and limit the number of passengers to reduce the risk of distraction.

Note* Stimulant medications are often used to improve driving performance in those with ADHD.

- **Sticking to A Good Medication Regimen**

As teens get older, the age-old stigma of taking medication rears its ugly head. In some cases, teens feel they no longer need their medication and stop taking it regularly. If your teen decides to come off their medication, encourage them to do this under the guidance of a medical practitioner. Use this trial period to create coping strategies for your teen. Agree on specific factors that may indicate they need to go back on to their treatment. For example, poor grades, struggling at home, or socially.

- **Medication Diversion**

Giving away or selling prescription drugs is not a new thing. In the case of ADHD medication, the uses could be recreational or academic. Teens looking to get rid of their medication may give it away to friends and peers or sell it to gain access to cash. Explain to your teen that this is illegal and that the medication could have an adverse reaction if taken by someone who doesn't need it and isn't under any medical supervision.

- **Boosting Confidence & ADHD Disclosure**

Create a loving and supportive environment for your teen. Constantly remind them that you are there to help with the challenges they face and that you believe in them and their ability to achieve their dreams. Identify their strengths and shine the proverbial spotlight on their natural talents.

ADHD disclosure may not have been an issue in the past, but as your teen develops and matures, they may feel differently about this. Discuss this openly, benefits vs. risks regarding disclosure, and agree on a way forward that is acceptable to both sides.

- **Working For Your Teen's future**

With so much bad press about ADHD, it's no wonder many parents worry their beautiful teens are destined to be delinquents facing a dead-end adult future. In all honesty, yes, ADHD poses many 'challenges' for teens, and there are days when they 'strike out,' BUT these challenges don't define your teen. In fact, many teens go on to live full, productive, and balanced lives thanks to the relentless efforts of parents like you, continued awareness, and treatments available.

STRATEGIES FOR BUILDING TEEN EXECUTIVE FUNCTION

Teens, in general, have a lot to deal with, larger groups of friends, increased school pressures, schedules, and extracurricular activities. This, coupled with poor executive function skills, can impact learning ability, long-term planning, and goal setting.

The strategies below can help your teen flex their executive function muscles.

- Scaffold Scheduling, Deadlines, and Good Study Habits

Use a calendar or diary to keep track of assignments, tests, and projects. Create a work list and rank each task in order of priority to ensure work remains on track.

- Recognize Teen Pressure Points

Feeling emotionally safe is pivotal to successful learning. Research has shown that taking time out for self-reflection is as essential as putting in hours of study time. According to a 2015 study, positive self-talk such as 'I can do this' or 'I will do my best' breaks the association between negative self-belief and poor performance, resulting in improved academic achievement!

- Have Teens Write About It

While journaling with ADHD isn't easy because teens struggle to slow down, focus or make it a regular practice. Writing down their worries, thoughts, and feelings can help them gain perspective and build emotional resilience.

- Empower Teens

As parents, it can be frustrating to be ignored when giving advice regarding studies. Phrases like 'schedule time for daily revision' and 'put your phone on silent' are often disregarded. Switch things up by asking them to write a letter to themselves advising on suitable study measures. A 2019 study proved that students who wrote guidance to others about studying improved their own academic performance.

- Learning – Do It For The Greater Good

Struggling to get your teen to complete a task or take their studies seriously is the age-old war cry of every parent. A study conducted by researchers at the University of Pennsylvania concluded that unless students can see the correlation between how the task benefits them and others, it's often disregarded or considered boring. However, they spend more time on academic tasks when they learn to connect their learning to a higher purpose (reason beyond themselves).

- Interests, Passion & Community

Be interested in your teen, get to know their likes and dislikes, hopes and dreams. Encourage them to speak up and have opinions about current events and other issues. Use games, art, or evening dinners as the time to chat about the stuff that matters. Encourage your teen to get involved in community projects or volunteer. According to a 2014 study conducted by David Yeager, students (teens) who have a sense of self and purpose are better placed to define their goals and remain focused.

ACTIVITIES FOR EXECUTIVE FUNCTIONING IN TEENS

▷ **Goal-setting, Planning & Monitoring**

Self-regulation & Cognitive Flexibility

Encourage your teen to identify things they would like to do or achieve. This could be planning a birthday party or saving for a new computer game. Then, as they gain more confidence in the planning process, they could tackle long-term goals like opening a bank account, purchasing a car, or applying to college.

Attentiveness & Impulse Control

Part of the planning process requires monitoring self-behavior. Remind your teen to check in with themselves regularly. Questions they could ask themselves include: Is my behavior helping my plans? Are these plans going to achieve my goals? If not, why am I doing this? Has anything changed? Using a diary to keep track of this self-monitoring can help slow things down and provide time for focus and reflection.

Focus, Attention & Cognitive Flexibility

Help your teen develop strategies and plans to achieve their goals. This could be as simple as preparing for a test or practicing for a team event. Planning ahead and anticipating possible issues that may arise is excellent practice for cognitive flexibility.

▷ **Tools For Self-Monitoring**

Focus, Working Memory, Self-Regulation

Self-talk, or as I call it (pep-talk), is an excellent way for teens to turn their thoughts into courageous and enthusiastic action! Talking to themselves as they work through challenging tasks can make the task seem more manageable and encourage focus and attention. This strategy can also be used when dealing with negative feelings and emotions as it helps teens recognize when they are internalizing issues. At this point, I always encourage my son to include positive affirmations in his self-talk, such as 'I can do this' or 'I am not a failure.'

▷ **Self-awareness, Attention, And Focus**

Journaling provides teens with a safe space to explore their emotions, thoughts, and feelings. It also encourages planning, decision-making, and focus.

▷ **Sports And Games**

Self-Regulation & Cognitive Flexibility

Active sports such as soccer, volleyball, or hockey promote self-regulation and the ability to monitor the actions of others. They also encourage quick decisions and responses based on the movements of their teammates and the opposing side.

Mindfulness & Self-awareness

Mindful meditation and yoga are excellent stress relievers that encourage conscious awareness. The slow controlled movements and focused breathing techniques seen in these activities can help teens develop focus, reduce explosive reactions and encourage calm decision-making and behaviors.

Working Memory, Cognitive Flexibility & Inhibition

Learning to play complicated music pieces, dance, and singing routines that involve multiple parts and improvisation challenges and develops core executive function skills.

▷ **Study Skills**

Basic organizational skills are essential to support executive function skills. Use the below as a quick guide to help manage school workloads.

- Split assignments and projects into manageable portions.
- Develop a plan with timelines that identifies the steps required to complete the task.
- Self-monitor regularly, check-in, or set a timer to ensure focus and understanding are maintained. Check notes and ask for help if things are going off course.
- Turn off distractions such as phones, tablets, or tv. Ensure the study area is quiet.
- Use a calendar or vision board to keep track of deadlines and important information.
- Consider possible improvements. Spend time assessing how the assignment went and what can be improved for future tasks.

Parenting a teen with ADHD can feel like an uphill struggle. The extra work, dedication, and stamina required are nothing short of super-human! However, ADHD doesn't have to be the stigma society suggests. My son is a testament to this fact. If I can offer only one line of advice, it's this. Pick your battles wisely, accept the easy wins and learn to pack away the combat gear; it's not always necessary.

5
THERE'S A PROBLEM. WHAT'S THE SOLUTION?

"Every great and deep difficulty bears in itself its own solution. It forces us to change our thinking in order to find it."

— NIELS BOHR

When it comes to problems, "I'm no shrinking violet," as my mother used to say. My usual course of action is to roll up my sleeves and get busy FIXING it. Unfortunately, accepting help is not something I find easy to do, and as a result, I'm often found burning the proverbial candle at both ends. As fellow ADHD parents, you know this doesn't bode well for effective parenting, especially ADHD parenting. Tired parents plus ADHD kids' equal nuclear disaster!

Striving to be a good parent when faced with the daunting leer of ADHD can leave you wondering how on earth you will cope, but the funny thing about situations like these is that there is always help on hand. You just need to know where to look for it and realize that accepting help isn't admitting defeat to this chronic condition.

This chapter will highlight some of the remedies and respites available to fantastic parents such as yourself. However, please remember many of these so-called solutions have been devised based on medical science rather than parental input. As a parent, you spend the most amount of time with your child. You understand their triggers, challenges, and fears. Most of all, you are in sync with their unique personality traits and quirks. My point is, you know your child better than anyone else ever could and are therefore better placed to make decisions regarding their ADHD treatments.

Furthermore, some remedies may work perfectly for some kids but not for others. Remember that ADHD doesn't turn your child into a carbon copy of other kids with the same condition. Each child is unique, and it's this individuality that should determine the best approach for their treatment or coping strategies. Of course, these should be guided not only by those Ph.D.-waving professionals but also by you, the fantastic parents who quite literally hold their kids together on a daily basis!

POSSIBLE TREATMENT OPTIONS FOR ADHD

ADHD is commonly treated with stimulant medications; however, these are not a cure, simply a way to relieve the condition's symptoms and help manage daily life. Treatment is usually prescribed by a medical professional, and often a combined approach of medication and behavioral therapies is used. Unfortunately, there is a lot of negativity attached to ADHD medications.

Some believe that ADHD medications are used to manage normal behavioral issues, but you know your child and are better placed to make this decision. Furthermore, if you decide the medication route is not for your child, the simple strategies in this book will help you transform your parenting skills and reduce the effects of ADHD. That's not to say you can't use these strategies alongside medication; ADHD requires access to a full complement of artillery!

Medicine

- Methylphenidate

This stimulant drug increases brain activity in areas that control attention and behavior.

- Lisdexamfetamine

Lisdexamfetamine stimulants can improve focus and concentration and reduce impulsivity.

- Dexamfetamine

This stimulant is similar to Lisdexamfetamine and also improves attentiveness and inhibition.

- Atomoxetine

Atomoxetine increases the brain chemical noradrenaline. It aids with impulse control and concentration.

- Guanfacine

Guanfacine stimulates brain activity in areas that control attention.

SIDE EFFECTS OF MEDICATION

As with all medications, ADHD stimulants can have some nasty side effects. It's best to be aware of these as I firmly believe that knowledge is power and understanding the effects these drugs could have will help you make an informed decision.

Methylphenidate

- Headaches
- Stomach aches
- Loss of appetite
- Sleep issues
- Increased (minimal) heart rate and blood pressure
- Aggression, anxiety, depression

Lisdexamfetamine

- Nausea/vomiting
- Diarrhea
- Dizziness
- Aggression
- Reduced appetite
- Drowsiness
- Headaches

Dexamfetamine

- Decreased appetite
- Headaches
- Mood swings
- Agitation
- Aggression
- Diarrhea
- Nausea/vomiting

Atomoxetine

- Irritability
- Depression
- Suicidal Thoughts
- Headaches
- Stomach aches
- Disturbed sleeping patterns
- Nausea/vomiting
- Dizziness
- Increased (minimal) heart rate and blood pressure

Guanfacine

- Dry mouth
- Headaches

- Stomach aches
- Fatigue/tiredness

The right dosage is vital for minimizing the side effects associated with ADHD medications. Stimulant medications work by increasing norepinephrine and dopamine (brain chemicals). When these levels are correct, kids become focused; however, if the balance is off, it can have adverse side effects.

WHAT CAUSES SIDE EFFECTS?

Aside from getting the dosage right, timing and the length of time the medication is active can also cause negative side effects. For example, some stimulants are fast acting while others are slow releasing. ADHD medications typically last between 4 and 14 hours, depending on the type of stimulant taken.

Sometimes the sleep issues seen with medication are caused because it is still 'active' in the body at bedtime. Also, problems with appetite are usually seen after the medication has started working. Most professionals suggest eating a good breakfast before the medication begins to work and then a healthy dinner when the drugs are wearing off.

While the list of side effects looks like a long shopping list of issues, it's important to remember that not all children experience ALL of these side effects. Each child is unique in their response to medication.

GOLDEN RULES FOR ADHD MEDICATIONS

- Store in a childproof container – overdose can be serious/fatal.
- Supervise medication – children or teens should not manage the medicines without adult supervision.
- Deliver medicine directly to the school – supplies should not be sent with children.

It's imperative that parents supervise and manage medications to ensure the correct dosage is taken appropriately. This ensures that they are effective and safely administered and managed.

Therapies

Therapy can also treat ADHD symptoms and co-occurring conditions such as anxiety or behavior issues.

Psychoeducation

As the name suggests, it is a form of education. Parents and children with ADHD discuss the diagnosis, symptoms, and effects of the condition on school and family life with a professional. Psychoeducation helps you find ways of coping and living with ADHD.

Behavior Therapy

Behavior therapy is used to identify and change unhealthy behavior patterns in both adults and children. While it complements ADHD treatments, behavior therapy is also used to treat other co-occurring conditions such as anxiety, depression, OCD, and substance abuse disorders.

Several types of therapy fall under the umbrella of behavior therapy; these include:

- Cognitive behavioral therapy

Cognitive therapy focuses on the thoughts and actions of individuals. Its two-part approach aims to identify how your thoughts and beliefs influence your actions. Treatment is centered around current issues in your life and how you can resolve them. This type of therapy is a powerful long-term approach that develops healthy thought patterns and behaviors.

- Cognitive behavioral play therapy

This is a standard treatment for children with mental health conditions. By watching the child play, the therapist can assess the child's ability to express themselves and how they prefer doing this. Parents are taught how to use this information to improve communication with their children and help them cope and achieve their goals.

- Acceptance and commitment to therapy

Also known as ACT, this therapy focuses on language and mental processes. With the guidance of a mental health professional, individuals are taught to use mindfulness, behavioral change, and other strategies to increase psychological flexibility.

- Dialectical behavioral therapy

Usually used to treat borderline personality disorders, DBT can also be used to treat the co-occurring conditions of ADHD, such as depression, anxiety, etc. It uses four modules to teach skills and coping strategies; these include:

◇ Distress tolerance
◇ Emotion regulation
◇ Mindfulness
◇ Interpersonal skills (improve relationships)

Aside from behavior therapies and medications, parenting a child with ADHD should be based on the building blocks of basic parenting. These are consistency, patience, and positivity. If you are consistent, clear, and focused, reward and provide praise for positive behavior and firm but kind when meeting out consequences, the effect on your child's behavior will be nothing short of amazing!

PARENT TRAINING & EDUCATION PROGRAMS

As parents, we are supposed to have all the answers, at least that's what society dictates. However, this couldn't be further from the truth. An ADHD diagnosis literally blows standard parenting tactics right out of the water and can leave you confused about how to help your child. This is why behavioral management training for parents can provide vital skills and coping techniques that can be used to improve your child's behavior and soothe the ADHD storm at home.

BPT (Behavioral Parent Training) programs teach parents like us to help our kids behave better. Training is overseen by a mental health professional and covers the following aspects of parenting:

- Home rules and routine
- Organization
- Providing clear instruction
- Forward planning
- Managing kids in public spaces
- Praise/reward systems
- Ignoring mild behavior indiscretions

Training programs are also used to help parents develop techniques for teens with ADHD.

As parents with kids who have ADHD, it's essential to be well informed about the condition, its symptoms, causes, treatments, and the ways you can support your kids at home and school. Organizations such as CHADD or The U.S Department of Educations Office of Special Education Programs provide information, training, and online support for parents.

SOCIAL SKILLS TRAINING

Children who have ADHD often struggle in social situations. Reading the reactions and social cues of others is extremely difficult, and as a result, they may find social interactions demoralizing. Social skills training focuses on practicing appropriate responses and behaviors in a social setting. Training is overseen by a therapist who teaches children how to interpret the cues of others and respond in an acceptable manner.

HEALTH & DIET FOR KIDS WITH ADHD

All parents want to see their children clear their dinner plates. From the first day we hold them in our arms, providing them with the best diet becomes an almost OCD tendency amongst us parents! This is not a bad thing; after all, we want our kids to be healthy and grow well, it's a parental thing, and it goes with the territory. There's nothing more satisfying than watching those carrots and beans disappear off their plates! Okay, mom, goggles off!

- Nutrition is complementary, not the cure

Nutrition, no matter how good it is, is not going to cure ADHD. It can, however, help manage its symptoms. The brain and entire body require a balance of protein, healthy fats, carbohydrates, and nutrients to function optimally. So, it stands to reason that good nutrition complements ADHD treatments (medication & therapy).

Avoid empty calories found in cookies, chips, and candy and instead offer healthy foods that include dairy, protein, fruit, and vegetables.

- Special diets 50/50

Diets such as the Keto diet are often thought to improve ADHD symptoms. While there has been some research done into whether restrictive diets are beneficial, the results were marginal and not found to be helpful for every child.

Instead of removing foods, incorporate healthy, nutrient-rich foods. If you suspect your child has a food allergy or food sensitivity, seek advice from your doctor to avoid nutrient deficiencies and unhealthy weight loss.

- Be curious and vigilant about additives

Sugar and artificial additives such as food dye have long been the scapegoats for ADHD behavior issues. While this may be true for some children, not all children have the same response to these ingredients.

Diets that are rich in sugar and processed foods can also affect kids without ADHD. To be honest, reducing the amount of sugar and processed foods we consume is beneficial to everyone, not just kids with ADHD!

- ADHD medications can affect appetite

Weight loss and nutrient deficiency are some of the side effects of taking ADHD medications. This isn't down to poor parenting but rather because the medication suppresses their appetite. Usually, this returns when the drug wears off.

Ensure your child has access to nutritious foods before taking the medication and when it wears off. In addition, provide small healthy snacks throughout the day, smoothies, or nutritional health shakes to optimize their nutrient intake.

NUTRIENTS & SUPPLEMENTS FOR ADHD

The brain requires a good supply of nutrients to function well. This should include foods that provide healthy fats, proteins, and carbohydrates.

Let's look at the nutrients required for healthy brain function and good health.

- Polyunsaturated Fats (Omega-3)

Found in: Salmon, tuna, nuts, spinach, canola oil & supplements

While further research is needed, it is thought that Omega-3 (fatty acids) such as EPA and DHA can improve blood circulation in the brain. They may also improve ADHD symptoms such as hyperactivity, impulsivity, and attention.

- Magnesium

Found in: nuts, seeds, whole grains, beans

A diet rich in magnesium may help with attention and focus. In addition, magnesium is known for the calming properties it has on nerves and muscles.

- Iron

Found in: beans, leafy greens, meat, and meat products

Iron is vital for oxygen circulation throughout the body and cognitive development. Symptoms of iron deficiency include fatigue, low immunity, sleep disturbances, and difficulty learning.

- Zinc

Found in: Milk, beef, beans, and fortified breakfast cereals! (Win for Lina!)

Zinc is vital for brain development and other nerve activity in the brain. Inattentiveness has been linked to Zinc deficiency, as has poor health and appetite. Supplements are also an excellent option to increase zinc intake if a deficiency is suspected.

ELIMINATION DIET FOR ADHD

There is a lot of debate around whether elimination diets work for ADHD. Some sciency gurus promote it; others don't. However, a review published in 2017 showed there wasn't enough evidence to suggest that such diets could treat ADHD.

Think about this logically, if you followed a diet that increased energy levels but didn't sustain these throughout the day. The subsequent crash in energy may impact things like mood and irritability. In addition, being hungry and tired affects ADHD symptoms; just ask any parent struggling with the ensuing chaos caused by tiredness and ADHD combined!

Most of my research into elimination diets and their benefits for ADHD suggests that following a healthy, balanced diet is a more practical approach rather than drastic elimination diets. However, if you feel this is an option you want to explore further, there are a few things to consider.

- Speak to your doctor/nutritionist first; they can advise if an elimination diet is best for your child's current health conditions.
- Ensure your child receives a balanced diet that provides essential vitamins, minerals, and calories.
- Go slow; eliminate one thing at a time to see what works

Treating ADHD is a complex process or, as I like to say, war strategy. It requires a balanced and pragmatic approach to medication, behavioral therapies, and diet. Often parents get hung up on one form of treatment, hoping that it will be the answer to their prayers. Unfortunately, ADHD doesn't conform to the 'one size fits all' thought process.

Because your child is unique, you may find the treatments mentioned in this chapter don't work for your child. However, with patience and the super parenting strategies I have put together for you, discovering the right balance and remedy that works for you and your beautiful child will be much easier.

6

HANDLING THE EMOTIONAL DISTRESS

"The Scars You Can't See Are The Hardest To Heal."

— UNKNOWN

What does it mean to be a parent? I was asked this question by my grandmother when she first heard I was pregnant with my eldest son. I remember thinking about it for a few minutes before rattling off a list of duties, most of which involved providing adequate care such as food, clothing, and a home. My Grandmother is quite a wise lady; she simply smiled and said, "Lina, you have a lot to learn," and she was right. As a newbie parent, I had no idea about most things relating to parenthood. Until that first day, when holding his tiny hand in mine, I realized what she had been trying to convey.

While parenting does involve a lot of clean-up duty, it also involves providing protection. As I held that tiny hand for the first time, I realized that above all things, I wanted to protect this tiny human from every possible threat, perceived or otherwise. I wanted to wrap him in cotton wool – protect him from the slightest bump or hardship. Because being a parent meant being the ULTIMATE protector.

Unfortunately, wrapping our kids in cotton wool isn't something that life allows, and sadly, they are exposed to many outside influences that can potentially affect their development and mental health. Believe me, in most cases, this isn't down to bad parenting. Unfortunately, sometimes things happen beyond our control, and no matter how much we want to protect them, the resulting scars are not easily dispensed with. This can lead to emotional distress and subsequent behavioral problems that can exacerbate or mimic ADHD symptoms if not understood.

Sadly, emotional distress can be caused by a number of things, many of which we as parents strive to protect our kids from experiencing. Perhaps your child grew up or is currently living in a distressed environment?

This could further aggravate their ADHD. As parents, we can help them cope and overcome the emotional distress they are struggling with by using some basic strategies.

COPING STRATEGIES

Even though many people associate ADHD as an excuse for badly behaved children, this couldn't be further from the truth. Kids with ADHD can learn right from wrong just as well as any other child. However, the way they do this may need to be adjusted to suit their unique needs. Here's some simple advice courtesy of me, Lina Cole, a veteran in the below parental coping strategies.

The poor impulse control seen in kids with ADHD is often the cause of poor behavior patterns. Recognizing this root cause and its effects on brain function will turn your standard parenting approach into one bespoke to your child. As you learn to adapt and change how you interact with your child, you can turn your parenting style into a positive and rewarding experience.

Keep in mind that factors such as physical environment, language, gestures, and speech all directly impact your child's behaviour. In addition, kids with ADHD benefit from structure and consistency; when you get all of these ingredients right, the challenging behaviors you are struggling with today will soon be a thing of the past.

1. Structure

Daily schedules are excellent for calming the ADHD storm. Sticking close to a routine that manages different aspects of their lives, waking up, getting ready for school, eating, and doing homework, takes the stress out of sudden distractions.

2. Keep them Interested

Kids with ADHD can either struggle with distractibility (lack of focus) or hyperfocus (overly focused). While distractibility happens when the task is not challenging enough, hyperfocus is when they become absorbed and unaware of their surroundings. Encourage tasks or hobbies that require focus but are also challenging enough to keep them interested.

3. Praise & Recognition

Praise and recognition are often in short supply for kids with ADHD. Their lives are based on correction and complaints about their behavior in school and other settings. Therefore, it's vital that, as parents, we use praise to reinforce good behavior. This will encourage them to repeat these behaviors and help to differentiate between acceptable and unacceptable behavioral expectations. Remember, a few drops of human kindness are an oasis in a desert of criticism.

4. Encourage Good Sleep Patterns

Poor quality sleep can impact ADHD symptoms. Encourage a regular bedtime that provides adequate rest. Good sleep patterns improve mood and increase energy levels.

5. Simplify Requests & Tasks

Complex tasks can represent an impossible challenge for kids with ADHD. As a result, they may put things off and avoid completing them. The task can seem less daunting by breaking down the request or task into 'bite-sized' chunks. For example, if part of their chores is to clean the kitchen, it could be broken down into stacking the dishwasher, wiping the counters, sweeping the floor, and packing excess food away.

6. Explain

Use positive language to explain your reasoning behind requests. This removes the doubt and confusion felt by kids with ADHD. Keep the explanation simple and your instruction clear. When we take time to explain things to our children, it engenders mutual respect, which is especially important for kids with ADHD who may already feel inadequate and different from their peers.

7. Avoid Negative Feedback

We're all human and being positive in the face of ADHD adversity can leave you highly stressed and frustrated. While constructive criticism has its place, if we constantly focus on the things our kids get wrong, using hurtful language, it can leave them feeling deflated and cause poor behavior to worsen.

Instead of allowing these feelings to overflow into your communication with your child, speak to a close friend, family member, therapist, or support group. This can provide you with the space to express your concerns and frustrations and find relief interacting with others in similar situations.

8. Split Second Rule

Kids with ADHD struggle with impulse control. This can cause them to say or act inappropriately. Encouraging them to stop for a split second before acting or speaking gives them time to process and consider whether their words or actions are an appropriate response. This is especially beneficial for their social interactions with others.

9. Combat vs Peace

Hyperactive and impulsive behavior can be tricky to manage daily. As parents, we want the best for our kids; however, if we constantly micro-manage (I'm speaking from personal experience here) and scrutinize each minor issue, it can cause a significant amount of friction. Learning to let the little things slide (hang up your combat boots) can help you focus on more important behavioral problems and relieve the stress felt by both you and your child.

However, although minor allowances should be made, ADHD shouldn't be an excuse for bad behavior. Boundaries are important and consistent consequences for misbehavior are essential; if these are not in place, they could encourage negative behaviors to continue.

10. Practice Self-care

Caring for a child with ADHD can be physically and mentally exhausting. If you don't care for yourself, your parenting skills will eventually suffer. Take regular breaks, hire a babysitter or ask a close friend or family member to watch your child.

Taking time to rest increases your ability to deal with stress. A calm parent is vital when faced with the raging beast of ADHD. Instead, incorporate a few of the below ideas into your daily routine to soothe and enhance your inner ADHD zen.

- Limit alcohol/caffeine intake
- Practice mindfulness
- Yoga/exercise are excellent stress relievers
- Go for walks in nature
- Set up a daily routine
- Be kind to yourself
- Prayer (My personal favorite)

ADHD & EMOTIONS

Kids with ADHD experience the same emotions as any other person without ADHD. The difference comes in with how they regulate these emotions. While young kids without ADHD are generally unruly and excitable, they learn to control and manage these emotions as they mature. Kids with ADHD find this skill (self-regulation) challenging, and it often leaves them struggling to express their emotions appropriately. As a result, you may notice they struggle with some or all of the following:

- Struggle to cool off after becoming upset
- Worry or become frustrated about minor things
- Impatience
- See gentle criticism as a direct attack/insult

However, this can also swing the other way, and some kids may find it challenging to regulate feelings of excitement or expectation. As you can see, emotions can be incredibly confusing for children with ADHD; this confusion and lack of self-regulation causes outbursts or withdrawal from others. However, as parents, we can help them get a handle on their emotions with patience and by following a few simple rules.

GOLDEN RULES FOR ENHANCING EMOTION CONTROL

- Listen – provide them with the space to express how they are feeling.
- Empathize – a sympathetic ear is an excellent calmative.
- Validate – try not to undermine their feelings. While their emotions may not make sense at times, they are very real to your child.

ADHD & ANGER – THE CONNECTION BETWEEN THE TWO

One of the primary symptoms of ADHD is impulsivity which inhibits the ability to concentrate or control behaviors; in other words, self-regulate. This means that kids with ADHD act on their feelings immediately; things like anger and frustration are expressed straight away. This is called impulsive aggression and is common among children with ADHD as it causes unplanned emotion or aggression in stressful situations.

ADHD doesn't take emotions away; instead, it tends to magnify them disproportionately. In addition, co-occurring conditions such as ODD, anxiety, impulsive aggression, and medication side effects, when added to the already volatile ADHD mix, create the perfect recipe for aggressive outbursts, impatience, and anger.

MOODINESS AND MOOD DISORDERS

ADHD can have many 'emotional faces' throughout the day, from happiness to frustration, sadness to anger, and that's just before breakfast! Often children with ADHD are at risk of other mood disorders such as depression, bipolar or anxiety disorders; these can further increase anger, mood change, and irritability. Below are some factors that may affect your child's mood throughout the day.

- Hyperactivity (physical/verbal)

Hyperactivity can sometimes be too hard to control; after all, kids with ADHD are only human. In my home, we call this the 'volcano effect'. As with lava, sometimes the only place for feelings and emotions is 'up', causing angry outbursts and physical aggression.

- Poor Self-esteem

Academic ability and social interactions can present a significant challenge for kids with ADHD. Unfortunately, underachievement and loneliness can leave your child feeling isolated or deflated and result in feelings of anger because these situations are beyond their control.

- Stimulant Side Effects

ADHD medications are stimulants which, as they wear off, may cause your child to become moody, angry, or have a full on melt-down. This is called medication rebound and is the term used for the speed at which your child's body metabolizes (processes) the medication.

If you notice your child is struggling with anger and irritability when the medication is wearing off, speak to your medical practitioner. Usually, a short-acting medication is prescribed to help soothe the transition period.

ODD AKA OPPOSITIONAL DEFIANT DISORDER

ODD is a psychiatric disorder that causes challenging behaviors and emotional outbursts. This condition causes full-on defiance and purposeful misbehavior no matter what the consequence. As you can imagine, ODD can negatively impact the already volatile symptoms of ADHD!

Typical symptoms include:

- Being argumentative
- Defies authority/ teachers/parents
- Not listening to instructions or requests
- Purposeful misbehavior/irritation of others
- Lying
- Causes conflict with peers and adults
- Easily angered/moody/annoyed
- Little empathy for others/vindictive or spiteful
- Frequent, volatile temper tantrums

These behaviors are usually demonstrated at school, home, and other settings. While kids without ADHD can also display some form of defiance towards their parents, this doesn't usually affect other environments.

There are two types of ODD these include:

Childhood ODD - presents at a young age, but treatments can help prevent it from developing into a severe conduct disorder.

Adolescent ODD – presents suddenly during teenage years and causes conflict at home and school.

I found it rather frightening to discover that one-third of children with ADHD also have ODD. As if there wasn't enough to deal with already? Furthermore, this can be extremely challenging to deal with on your own, and if left untreated, it can develop into a serious conduct disorder. Most treatments involve therapy, parent training, and medication for co-existing conditions such as ADHD, mood disorder, and anxiety.

SYMPTOMS OF EMOTIONAL DISTRESS

Emotional distress can negatively impact almost every aspect of our lives, from how we interact with others to the foods we eat, the amount of sleep we get, and how we see ourselves. Most of us will experience some form of emotional distress in our lives caused by stressful situations. However, for us, the symptoms eventually dissipate and are considered temporary.

However, in some cases, emotional distress symptoms can develop into mental health disorders, meaning symptoms remain for long periods and may require treatment.

Symptoms of Emotional Distress

- Poor appetite or overeating
- Insomnia or excessive sleeping
- Low self-esteem
- Low energy
- Poor concentration

- Feelings of hopelessness

The causes of emotional distress (emotional suffering) vary from one person to the next. They can range from a traumatic event to a mental health condition such as bipolar, depression, or anxiety.

THE LINK BETWEEN ADHD AND CHILDHOOD TRAUMA

Childhood trauma is a psychological reaction to a distressing or disturbing event. This could be something that physically happened to them or the result of witnessing something happens to someone or something else. The effects this has on the brain, and its development can negatively impact their emotions and behaviors, causing concentration and self-regulation issues similar to ADHD.

I'm not saying your child has definitely experienced a dramatic event in their life which is the reason for their ADHD. However, scientists have noted that ADHD and childhood trauma affects the same brain areas, hence their similarities.

Because of this similarity in symptoms, childhood trauma could easily be confused with ADHD leading to a misdiagnosis. Furthermore, studies have found that kids with ADHD are more likely to have experienced a traumatic event than those without ADHD.

SHARED ADHD & CHILDHOOD TRAUMA SYMPTOMS

- Disturbed sleep patterns
- Distractibility
- Inattentive
- Hyperactive
- Struggles to concentrate
- Learning difficulties
- Disorganized

The brain's prefrontal and temporal cortex regulates emotions, controls impulses, and helps with decision-making. It's this brain area that is affected by ADHD and childhood trauma. The negative impact seen by both conditions are difficulties with concentration, processing sensory information, and managing emotions.

Types of Traumatic Events

- Serious injury
- Life-threatening medical conditions
- Physical or sexual abuse

- Witnessing violent acts
- Neglect or abandonment
- Death of a loved one
- Natural disaster
- Poverty
- Divorce of parents
- Life-threatening medical conditions
- Car accident

CHILDHOOD TRAUMA VS ADHD: CASE STUDY

A study conducted by Dr. Nicole Brown found that exposure to trauma at a young age increases stress levels which may impair neurodevelopment. So often, scientific research seems to be filled with facts and figures. None of which seem relatable to our children. I needed to see this link between ADHD and childhood trauma in the flesh, and so in my search to find something tangible to validate the link, I stumbled across the story of Amanda Scriver.

Amanda Scriver is a well-known freelance journalist. Based in Toronto, you can easily find her on Instagram. But more than who she is or where she is based; is the fact she is living, breathing proof of the link between childhood trauma and ADHD. Her parents divorced when she was just three years old, and teachers suggested her inattentiveness was attention seeking and defiant.

Throughout her school years, she struggled with schoolwork, low self-esteem, poor concentration, emotional regulation, and impulsivity. Sound familiar? After doing her research, she noticed a correlation between the trauma she had experienced and her quite obvious ADHD symptoms. Speaking to her therapist, she found that it was a well-known fact that children exposed to traumatic events can have the same behavioral issues as those with ADHD. While one doesn't cause the other, their link is quite significant.

HOW TO HELP YOUR CHILD OVERCOME TRAUMA & STRENGTHEN EMOTIONAL REGULATION

Like most good things, a calm and happy child begins at home, that and chicken soup, of course, but that's another story! My point is, as parents, we are in the perfect position to help our kids overcome any trauma in their lives and manage their emotional distress. For me, the similarities between ADHD and emotional distress were too blatant to ignore.

Being the practical person I am, when faced with ADHD and the possibility of emotional distress, I used my standard 'belt n braces' approach, which is just 'Lina-code' for doing everything in my power as a parent to empower my son.

Using the below strategies, I focused on helping my son cope with his emotional pain and strengthen his emotional intelligence.

- Pay attention to their feelings

All emotions are integral to being human, including anger and sadness. Often these two emotions have a terrible reputation as if feeling angry or sad is a bad thing. In fact, all of our feelings, even the negative ones, are a normal and natural way to process and respond to situations. Encourage your child to talk about how they feel, and provide definite labels for each emotion, for example; I feel angry 'because' or 'I get frustrated when.'

Opening a dialogue between you and your child regarding their feelings and emotions provides a safe space to express their emotions rather than allowing them to build up and become explosive. Remember that fear is often the primary emotion hiding behind anger.

- Listen to them & hear them

If you are the parent of a teen with ADHD, you probably snorted into your tea when I suggested talking to them. Most teens find it difficult to talk about their feelings to their parents, even those without ADHD. Instead, encourage them to speak to a trusted friend, family member, or teacher; remember it's essential they keep talking, even if it isn't to you at the moment.

However, if your child does want to talk, take the time to really listen to them and hear what they are saying. This means stop what you are doing, folks, and focus on the conversation!

I say this because I know what it's like to be busy preparing dinner, trying to help with homework, shouting at the dog to get off the dinner table, and balancing a toddler on one hip while trying to 'listen' to something my son is trying to tell me. Consequently, I get distracted and frustrate him because he feels what he has to say isn't important enough.

Instead, take the time to sit down with your child or go for a walk and give them your undivided attention. Listen to their thoughts and feelings with empathy, and try not to judge, criticize or interrupt, as this promotes a healthy, healing relationship.

- Actively seek enjoyment

Encourage your child to focus on activities that bring enjoyment rather than focusing on the trauma. For example, playing games, reading, or watching a positive movie can help keep your child's mind occupied with uplifting things rather than the trauma's negativity. Create a space where your child has access to rest, play, and have fun. Connecting with simple pleasures such as nature walks, a trip to the local park, swimming, and playing catch can be extremely therapeutic for reducing emotional distress.

- Overriding impulses

Mindfulness and breathing exercises are methods that can be used to control the emotional rollercoaster caused by trauma. This, coupled with a good diet and healthy sleeping regime, enhances emotional intellect and impulse control while eliminating the classic knee-jerk reaction to stress caused by emotional distress.

◇ Mindfulness

Teaches your child to stop and focus on the present. As a result, they become more self-aware, less stressed, and calmer. This allows them to cope with their feelings and select appropriate responses to negative or unhelpful thoughts.

◇ Breathing

Our bodies automatically flick the 'flight of fight' mode switch when struggling with the stress of trauma. This triggers adrenaline and other chemicals, increasing heart rate and making breathing shallow. By learning to stop and take a deep breath, the body receives enough oxygen to help you relax and refocus.

- Believe in your child

As parents, we are responsible for providing a safe and secure place for our children to grow and develop. Unfortunately, this security is sometimes rocked by situations or circumstances beyond our control. Rebuilding their trust in themselves and the world around them takes time and a lot of patience.

Most importantly, they need to see that you believe they can overcome the emotional pain they are experiencing. Children tend to base their self-worth on the reactions and actions of those closest to them.

Parenting in a calm, positive and comforting manner ensures your child has the tools and appropriate environment in which to heal.

7

NURTURING SELF-ESTEEM

"Having A Low Opinion Of Yourself Is Not Modesty. Its Self-Destruction."

— BOBBY SOMMER

"It's a hot summer day, one of the hottest we've had in years. I'm standing on the front porch trying to encourage my son to join the other neighborhood kids running through the sprinkler on our front lawn. Clinging like a limpet to my leg, he refuses to look at the other kids, rushing through the spray and shrieking with delight. No matter how hard I try, I can't convince him to interact or join in the fun. He's convinced the other kids don't like him, the water looks cold, and he's scared the others will laugh at his new swimming trunks.

This information is delivered to me in a series of angry wails, frustrated flailing, and streams of hot angry tears. Eventually, in desperation, I gave up and took him inside to play with his lego. This happens every time I try to get him interested in something new."

The above diary excerpt is one I wrote when my son was very young. I remember I felt inadequate and believed I was failing as a parent. A confident child myself, I couldn't understand what had gone wrong; why did my son have such a different outlook on life? Was it my parenting or something else?

While every parent dreams of having a well-behaved, modest child capable of taking on the world and achieving all their dreams, this requires one simple ingredient – self-esteem. We can fight ADHD with medication, therapy, and coping strategies all we like, but our kids won't flourish without self-esteem. Fact.

Low self-esteem may see them struggle to participate in daily activities required for a balanced life, such as socializing and speaking to the opposite sex. This may not be a problem now while your child is young, and you can take them back indoors to play with their lego (exit left stage door, Lina Cole!), but it could prove detrimental to their adult lives, impacting their social skills and life choices.

SELF-ESTEEM IN CHILDREN

Positive self-esteem is crucial to every child's development, whether they have ADHD or not. It sets the scene for their social, emotional, and behavioral health and impacts how they deal with things like peer pressure, disappointment, and life's challenges. Use the below positive strategies to build your child's self-esteem.

- Recognizing True Self-esteem

When you look in the mirror, you see your reflection; self-esteem works in the same way, except it's an internal reflection that you see in your mind's eye. This is directly influenced by the amount of support or criticism children are exposed to by the people closest to them (parents, teachers, religious leaders, friends, extended family).

It's important to remember that healthy self-esteem is not about believing you are better than others or that your needs are more important than theirs. Therefore, it's crucial to balance self-esteem with the below essential life values.

> ◇ Good manners – teaches them to interact socially, respectfully, and politely
> ◇ Gratitude – teaches them to be thankful for the goodness in their lives
> ◇ Empathy – teaches them to understand and respect the feelings of others
> ◇ Charitable works – teaches them to help others and feel good about contributing toward positive change

- Unconditional Love & Quality Time

This seems an odd thing to suggest because, as parents, loving our kids is something we naturally do without consciously thinking about it. However, demonstrating this love is what I'm alluding to here. Express your love daily, hug them goodbye when leaving and spend quality time with them reading and cuddling. This daily affirmation of love will help them build solid and healthy relationships with others.

- Responsibility & Independence

Chores and responsibility provide children with a sense of achievement. This, in turn, builds confidence as they feel they are making a positive contribution. Select tasks appropriate for their ability, such as changing the pet's water bowl, sweeping the kitchen floor, or unpacking the dishwasher. Provide lots of positive feedback and encouragement. Encouraging independence is vital for self-esteem; it shows you believe in your child's abilities and teaches them they have the power over their choices and actions.

- Stop The Rage

We are all human and lose our tempers at times but yelling and name-calling simply shame your child into submission and teach them that aggression is a healthy form of communication! One thing kids with ADHD don't need is more aggression.

Name-calling can also be exceptionally damaging, especially as your child can start to believe the insults they are hearing. This can chip away at their perception of their self-worth and, ultimately, their self-esteem. Instead, speak calmly, and explain the consequences of their behavior. Consistency and patience are the key ingredients for calm parenting. If you find you are too angry to discuss the matter at first, take a walk to help you calm down. A calm parent is an effective parent.

- Failure Is An Opportunity To Learn

There's a phrase that loosely states, 'you learn from your mistakes,' which is especially true for kids. Mistakes or setbacks should be used as an opportunity to learn how to improve their behavior. This teaches them they are in control of their actions and can turn a somewhat negative situation into something positive. Failure addressed positively builds confidence and teaches them to 'pick themselves up' when mistakes happen rather than admitting defeat.

- Technology vs Family Time

While technology (phones, tablets, computers) is beneficial for homework, social media, and staying connected with friends, there's also the risk of it impacting communication and family relationships. For example, if a child spends too much time on their tablet or phone, it may interfere with exercise.

Exercise is vital for kids with ADHD needing to 'burn off' excess energy and promote good mental health. Instead, schedule time each day dedicated to off-screen activities such as reading, playing games, going for walks, or playing in the park.

- Showcase Their Creativity

Display your child's artwork or creative projects on the fridge or in a prominent part of the house. Providing children with the opportunity to discuss and show off their creativity teaches them that their thoughts and opinions matter and, you guessed it, exponentially promotes self-esteem!

- Healthy Risks Result In Effective Problem Solving

Healthy self-esteem is only possible if you allow your child to take healthy risks, make decisions, and take responsibility for their actions. If we rescue our children from every perceived failure, how will they learn to problem solve and become successful adults? Healthy risks could include going on a sleepover, walking to school, making their own breakfast (cereal & milk), or going on a roller coaster ride. Obviously, the types of risks they take should be age-appropriate and suited to their abilities.

WHAT CAUSES LOW SELF-ESTEEM IN CHILDREN?

The truth is kids with ADHD often struggle with low self-esteem. Things like struggling academically, bullying, and even childhood trauma directly impact a child's self-esteem. When I understood this, suddenly, the connection between self-esteem and ADHD made a lot of sense, especially as the effects of ADHD seemed to be the root cause of my son's poor self-perception.

- Academic Underachievement

Struggling to understand schoolwork, assignments, and failing tests can undermine a child's self-confidence. If they don't receive adequate support, they may start to believe they are unintelligent, fear failure, and question their self-worth.

- Performance Pressure

The world of technology has a lot to answer for when setting unrealistic goals for young people. Social media is peppered with fake role models who live wonderful lives in the perfect house and drive the perfect car while sporting a figure only an airbrush artist could achieve. My point is that when our kids can't achieve this level of perfection, it causes them to believe their efforts were a waste of time and that they have 'somehow' failed.

- Bullying

Bullying causes children and teens to develop a negative self-perception of themselves. This can affect their adult lives if they internalize and hold onto the pain. For example, being called fat, lazy or stupid can cause children to believe this is true and, in some cases, believe they deserve being called these names. But, of course, bullying isn't only name-calling; other forms of bullying could be physical intimidation, cyberbullying, and indirect bullying (spreading rumors).

- Loneliness

Busy family life, peer pressure, and struggling to fit in at school can all contribute to feelings of discomfort and loneliness. In addition, not spending enough time with our kids due to commitments and work pressures can also impact their self-esteem. Sometimes, children choose to isolate themselves if they are bullied or abused.

- Past Traumas

In the previous chapter, we discussed how past trauma can be linked to ADHD; the same is true for low self-esteem. Often children who have suffered trauma in the early developmental stages of their lives struggle with poor self-esteem. In most cases, they believe the trauma to be their fault or because they weren't 'worth' protecting. Examples of trauma include divorce, abusive parents/carers, accidents, witnessing violence, natural disasters, etc.

NARCISSISM AND ADHD... AND SOME THOUGHTS ON DAMAGE REPAIR

Acknowledging our part as parents in the ADHD chaos can be a bitter pill to swallow. No one wants to think that their parenting skills may directly or inadvertently contribute to their child's ADHD.

This is where some straight-talking is required, and you know me, it's my speciality. So, take a seat, get comfy; it's 'band-aid' removal time. In the previous chapter, we discussed that trauma could be linked to ADHD; many of their resulting symptoms are similar and affect the same brain area.

The reality is this. Sometimes trauma caused by poor parenting styles can directly impact a child's ADHD. Take a moment to absorb that statement. It's tough, I know; I've walked this same path, and accepting this is one of the hardest things to do. But before you close the book, thinking I'm playing the age-old blame game, hear me out.

I'm not suggesting your child's low self-esteem and ADHD is a result of bad parenting; sometimes, it's the unintentional mistakes or missed cues that hamper our children's confidence. Other times it's down to us our own personal issues that cause immense damage if we are not mindful of our actions while trying to teach our kids to behave and listen to us. As parents, we have the closest, most direct contact with our children, so it makes sense that our influence on their lives will have the most impact.

The quote "Physician, heal thyself" comes to mind, which means you need to heal yourself before attempting to heal others. This is so important when raising children, with or without ADHD. As parents, we need to acknowledge our own behaviors first before our parenting skills can be effective. That's not to say that those of us with medical conditions are poor parents; what I mean is we need a healthy foundation from which to work and the first step towards good parenting health is recognizing our own issues or conditions and taking proactive steps towards a life that is more rewarding for both you and your child.

To enumerate my point, I have chosen narcissism as an example of how our own health conditions may affect our parenting styles.

Narcissism (Narcissistic Personality Disorder) is a mental health condition in which the narcissistic person displays the following traits.

- Inflated sense of self-worth
- Lacks empathy for others
- Sees themselves as superior to others
- Overly boastful of achievements
- Easily angered or moody in the face of criticism
- Craves attention
- Fragile self-esteem

ADHD and narcissism are often confused because both conditions seem to affect a person's ability to display empathy towards others. While ADHD can cause issues with compassion towards others, it isn't a formal symptom of the condition, and not everyone with ADHD struggles with it. However, it is a classic symptom of narcissism.

Narcissism and ADHD in action:

It's helpful to understand how each condition affects a person's interactions with others when trying to differentiate between them.

For example, in the course of a conversation, someone with ADHD may struggle to focus, interrupt or seem disinterested due to issues caused by executive functioning. However, when conversing with someone who has NPD, the same behaviors may occur, but these are self-centered and not caused by poor EF skills. Furthermore, behaviors such as demanding attention and admiration from others, lacking compassion, and an inability to show interest in others are also very evident.

HOW NARCISSISM AFFECTS ADHD KIDS

As you know, parenting kids with ADHD requires a lot of patience, empathy, and focus. Unfortunately, a narcissistic parent doesn't typically display these qualities, so you can imagine the ensuing chaos caused by their inconsistencies, rage, constant criticism, manipulation, and authoritarianism! And that's the shortened 'shopping list' of narcissistic issues!

Obviously, these narcissistic issues will cause immense anxiety and stress for a child with ADHD, who requires a calm and sensitive environment in which to function. In addition, children with narcissistic parents often struggle with distractibility, a primary symptom of ADHD. This may affect academic performance and chip away at their self-esteem. Dysregulation (physiological disturbances) can also occur, leading to eating disorders, self-harm, substance abuse, and other negative behaviors.

Some children choose partners or friends in adult life that exhibit the narcissism they experienced or observed in their narcissistic parents. This last one is the most upsetting for me; as your child develops, you may notice they display narcissistic behaviors, especially as they transition from teens to adults. To me, this just sounds like the proverbial vicious circle; when will it stop? As the non-narcissistic parent, it stops with you.

COPING STRATEGIES FOR COPING WITH A NARCISSISTIC PARENT

Sadly, it's not often that narcissistic parents recognize the damaging impact they may be having on their children. Unfortunately, the inability to see that their issue affects their child's ADHD will probably not see them positively contributing to managing their child's condition.

However, while co-parenting with a narcissistic parent is extremely challenging, there are ways to buffer your child and help them cope with the negative impact of narcissism. It's time to stop the chaos, reinstate order and calm that ADHD storm.

- **Avoid gaslighting your own child**

Pretending that narcissistic behaviors are acceptable will confuse your child. For example, when your child tells you about an uncomfortable situation, you tell them that the narcissistic parent didn't mean what they said or did and does love them. Think about it. How can negative behavior be a sign of love?

I'm not suggesting you pretend the narcissistic parent is perfect, but rather than running the parent down, allow your child to speak to you and offer empathy and reassurance that it's not their fault. This provides your child with a safe space to express themselves.

- **Use the lofty skyscraper technique**

This technique is about 'pulling back' instead of speaking directly about the narcissistic parent; use more generic language. For example, instead of mentioning the parent (naming and shame-ing), use terms like 'some adults aren't good with communication' or 'it's not okay when that happens, it is hard having to deal with that.'

A child in this situation requires support and empathy; they don't need you to 'fix' anything (unless there are safety concerns); they need you to listen and validate their feelings. It also allows them to gain some perspective on the situation.

- **Keep in mind developmental issues**

Narcissistic parents struggle with every developmental stage of their children. Tedious routine and boring childcare tasks can be triggers; however, a moody back-chatting teen can also escalate narcissistic rages. Sadly the emotional needs of others are not the focus of a narcissistic parent, which means that as your child develops, the way you help your child cope with the narcissism will change.

- **Instill empathy in your home**

Make time for emotional conversations with your child. Discuss how they are feeling after the day, what were the highs and lows and how each made them feel. It's important to encourage emotional intelligence in your child, to teach them to identify their emotions and recognize how they feel in certain situations.

Read stories to younger children and ask them to identify how each character is feeling. For older kids, you could watch a movie together and discuss their emotions throughout the film or go for long walks where the conversation is open to anything and everything, no holds barred. This always encouraged my son to open up to me; providing a neutral space to talk can be extremely beneficial.

- **Teach self-regulation and self-soothing**

Learning to lose and lose graciously is an important life lesson every child needs to learn. A narcissistic parent would probably rage about losing a board game or blame others for their mistakes or misfortune. This isn't how you want your child to react to disappointments in life.

Instead, use simple techniques through play to teach them it's okay to lose sometimes. For example, play games (board games, card games, hide & seek, catch) and don't let them win intentionally. This may seem harsh and cause tantrums or tears but let them experience these emotions. As they learn to self-soothe and accept that winning isn't always possible, they will begin to accept that outbursts and negative behaviors are not the answer to life's challenges.

- **Be consistent**

Narcissism and structure are polar opposites when it comes to the smooth running of a household and maintaining the routine required for parenting kids with ADHD. As a result, often ADHD parenting strategies go out the window, or if you stand your ground and insist on adhering to the routine, you're seen as the 'spoilsport.' That can be tough to deal with on a daily basis, especially if you are left to manage things like homework, bedtime, dinner and other tasks that the narcissistic parent deems too stressful for them.

While kids often moan about routines, it actually makes them feel safe and secure. Having boundaries and routine in a chaotic home means they have something tangible to cling to, and who better than the 'spoilsport' parent who holds their lives together?

- **Consider therapy**

Therapy is an excellent way to ensure your child receives the support and tools to overcome the anxiety, guilt, anger, shame, and confusion they may be experiencing while coping with a narcissistic parent.

I would suggest choosing a therapist specializing in narcissism and considering therapy for yourself. It's unlikely that the narcissistic parent will agree to send your child for therapy due to the stigma surrounding it and the fact they will have no control over what they say during the session. In that case, going for therapy yourself can be helpful as you can obtain the necessary coping skills and feedback required to help your child.

Narcissism is an extreme example of how poor parenting skills can impact ADHD and self-esteem. However, sometimes other mental health issues such as depression, anxiety, and adult ADHD can also affect how we parent our children. It's essential to recognize that we as parents aren't truly the superheroes society expects us to be (even though we wish we were); we are human, have our failings, past traumas, and often need support. However, the superhero element comes in when we realize and accept, we need help and do something proactive about it.

8

HANDLING THE WRECKING BALL

"Strategy without process is little more than a wish list."

— ROBERT FILEK

I'd like to start this chapter off by saying my home was the original site of the ADHD wrecking ball. From the exterior, our house looked like any other suburban household, with whitewashed walls, a pretty creeper trailing along the fence, and a slightly untidy garden path littered with the usual paraphernalia of life. In other words, strewn with kids' bikes, balls, the odd skipping rope, and the dog's favorite chew toy.

However, the external suburban bliss that people most saw as they drove or walked past our yard was the fragile shell that hid our home's inner war zone! Long before I understood the importance of structure, rules, and boundaries, which are the three cornerstones of calm ADHD parenting, my home was ruled by this chronic condition.

It stalked the home's inner sanctum like a raging lion and frequently disturbed the peace with tantrums, aggression, whining, and defiance. As a result, I felt like a circus ringmaster, perpetually and ineffectually fending off the lion with the only defense mechanisms I owned – poor strategies, failed attempts at structure, and wishful thinking. Sometimes as parents, we lull ourselves into a false sense of security, believing that somehow things will rectify themselves, especially when faced with the insurmountable task of ADHD.

I longed for the calm environment of my friend's homes and frequently indulged in green-eyed parent envy when watching their kids behave like well-trained seal pups. Not that I wanted my son to jump through hoops or catch fish mid-air, but it would have been nice to hear yes instead of no on occasion or have him respond to a request without a full-blown argument or tantrum each time.

Life in my home was exhausting, and I'm ashamed to say I often felt defeated and filled with negative thoughts. Sometimes the very idea of going home and facing the chaos that reigned was enough to have me turn my car around and go back to work.

Not that I did, of course, but I'm sure, as the parent of an ADHD child, you understand why I felt this way. If this is how you feel and you're tired of struggling with behavior problems, this chapter will help you introduce strategies to tame the lion and create the calm environment you crave.

BEHAVIOR PROBLEMS & ADHD CHILDREN

The negative symptoms of ADHD include inattentiveness and hyperactivity. Kids with ADHD are also susceptible to other behavior issues, including anxiety, depression, and defiance. These added issues can negatively impact their behavior and ADHD symptoms. In addition, side effects of ADHD medications can further exacerbate behavior problems if not understood or recognized.

- **Lying**

Occasional lying to prevent consequences, get attention or improve self-perception is part and parcel of being a normal kid. The trouble starts when lying becomes a habitual behavior and coping mechanism used to deal with the frustration and low self-esteem linked to ADHD. Understanding why the lies are occurring in the first place will help you stamp out the root of the issue. Below are some examples of how lies might appear when parenting a child with ADHD.

> Sarah's mom tells her to come straight home after football practice because the family is having friends around for dinner. In her hurry to get out the door on time, she yells a cursory "Yes, Mom," and dashes out.
> After a busy day, she returns home nearly an hour late, having forgotten the reminder from this morning. Of course, her mother confronts her, but Sarah is adamant she never told her to come home on time. While most would agree Sarah is lying, the fact is she forgot, which isn't an honesty issue but likely a record-keeping or organization issue, aka poor executive function.

> John's inattentiveness (inability to focus on tasks) has resulted in a shopping list of incomplete homework assignments. Ashamed and afraid to discuss the problem with his parents, he hides his school report when it is sent home. Most

would say John is deceiving his parents and would be correct in saying his behavior requires a consequence, but the inability to complete tasks also requires ADHD-focused strategies to help and support John with his learning.

So often, the root cause of lies can be stamped out by learning to manage negative ADHD symptoms. Sometimes lies result from issues at school or with friends; these social or academic problems need to be identified and resolved to eliminate the safety net of lies being used. This could involve behavior therapies and ADHD-friendly support strategies to assist with organization and other homework-related skills.

Impulsivity and avoidance caused by ADHD can also cause kids to do things beyond their control or fib about tasks they haven't done, such as sneaking that extra cookie and then denying it when caught out or saying they have done their chores when in fact, they haven't. It's thought that 'magical thinking' is the link between ADHD and lying. This is where the individual believes their wishes influence actual events. For example, if they regret taking that cookie, then wishing it hadn't happened means it didn't.

However, in some instances, lies can become deliberate and malicious; this is when they need to be addressed with appropriate force and consistency. Parents should also consider the possibility of co-occurring conditions such as anxiety, depression, or behavioral disorders.

It's also quite common for children with ADHD to be diagnosed with Conduct Disorder (CD). Children with this condition may display negative behaviors, for example, being aggressive or abusive to others or animals, lying, stealing, breaking rules, and damaging property on purpose.

- **Defiance**

All kids test their boundaries as they mature. It typically happens at each milestone of their lives, uncontrollable toddler, terrible twos, independent fives, and so on, until they reach adolescence, where they sometimes test their limits to the extreme. Of course, with patience and consistency, they realize their boundaries are firmly in place, and so the behavior moderates (to a degree!)

Unfortunately, kids with ADHD soon realize the performance struggles they face at home, school, and other settings. Watching their peers achieve basic milestones while they battle to achieve the same goals with immense effort can lead to feelings of frustration and the belief that they are unintelligent or that the world around them is highly critical of their attempts. The perceived unfairness of their situation can cause them to be resentful and display defiant behaviors in retaliation and frustration.

When defiance becomes extreme, disorders such as ODD (Oppositional Defiant Disorder) should also be considered. Kids with ODD persistently act out, causing severe stress at home, school, or with classmates, and purposely defy anyone they feel is in a position of authority over them. Typical ODD symptoms are anger, irritability, vindictiveness, and argumentative behaviors. ODD is a common disorder that occurs alongside ADHD; it affects approximately fifty percent (half) of children struggling with ADHD.

- **Too much screen time**

Before the days of technology, kids spent most of their day playing outside, reading, riding their bikes, and even climbing trees. Nowadays, the average kid spends most of this time in front of a screen. This could be a phone, tablet, computer, or even a tv screen.

Resisting the limits set for screen time can also be a behavioral problem that parents struggle to manage, especially if their kid's go-to reaction is tantrums and screaming. While it may seem easier to cave and give in to their screen time demands, too much time spent staring at a screen can seriously impact your child's ADHD symptoms.

Too much screen time can impact:

⋄ Social and emotional issues
⋄ Attention problems
⋄ Obesity from inactivity
⋄ Academic issues
⋄ Disturbed sleep cycles caused by the light off the screen
⋄ Aggression caused by exposure to violent films/video games

As you can see, the above issues caused by excessive screen time are very similar to symptoms of ADHD, for example, learning difficulties, disturbed sleep patterns, and attention issues. Therefore, too much screen time could worsen ADHD symptoms and should be monitored/limited.

If the thought of screaming tantrums caused by limiting screen time, has you ready to run in the opposite direction, don't panic, I have some strategies for dealing with this a little later in the chapter.

- **Food-related problems**

Picky eating, selective eating, or even overeating are demanding issues for any child to manage. Adding ADHD to this recipe can trigger further impulsivity, hyperactivity, lack of sleep, and irritability. Who knew that one green pea could be the reason for World War three! The cause of this could be down to sensory issues or a negative association with eating; stimulant medications can also cause a decrease in appetite.

Low dopamine levels also mean that kids with ADHD naturally crave sugary foods that deliver the boost (sugar high) their brain is demanding. Unfortunately, healthy foods such as fish and vegetables don't deliver this sugary boost, and as a result, healthy foods are often refused.

Of course, children with food-related issues aren't the kids who sometimes refuse to eat their vegetables. On the contrary, picky eaters tend to limit their food intake, refuse to try new foods (age-old breakfast cereal wars in the Cole household), and strongly dislike particular foods. However, other kids may claim they are always hungry and sneak food between meals. Binge eating or under eating can cause serious body image issues and need to be carefully and sensitively addressed.

- **Whining**

There's nothing more exhausting than dealing with a child who constantly begs, pleads, or repeatedly asks for the same thing, even though they have clearly heard the word no. Unfortunately, for parents, whining is typical behavior in all children, including those with ADHD. They may do this for attention, even if that attention is negative, and if it gets them what they want, it can develop into a bad habit that could continue into adult life.

Sadly, giving into whining for the sake of peace only reinforces that poor behavior gets them positive results. Learning to accept disappointment and other uncomfortable emotions such as anger and sadness are essential life skills all children need to learn. Whining and other negative behaviors such as aggression or sulking should not be seen as a way for them to regulate these emotions. Teaching our kids to understand and deal positively with uncomfortable situations rather than whining about them will help to reduce behavior issues.

- **Impulsive behavior**

ADHD is often associated with impulsive behavior (acting without thinking); this is also fairly common in young children without ADHD. They may do and say things without thinking, such as crossing the road without looking or saying inappropriate and hurtful things. However, most kids learn to self-regulate, and impulsive actions settle.

With ADHD, strong emotions and poor self-control result in impulsive actions ranging from physically lashing out, saying hurtful things, and making poor decisions regarding food, finances, schoolwork, and even safety.

- **Bedtime struggles**

It's common in most households to struggle with bedtime warzones at some point when raising kids. Refusing to go to bed on time and getting up frequently can be particularly frustrating for parents trying to establish a healthy sleep routine.

ADHD further impacts these frustrations as kids with this condition often battle with insomnia, sleep disorders, and RLS (Restless Leg Syndrome). In addition, difficulty waking up after disturbed sleep or extreme drowsiness after a poor night's sleep also affects cognitive function and attentiveness.

Sleep deprivation can increase behavioral issues, worsen ADHD symptoms without appropriate intervention, and impact physical health.

- **Aggression**

Most kids struggle to regulate their emotions when they are young; however, aggressive episodes tend to decrease as they develop and mature. Kids with ADHD find it difficult to manage their feelings and may verbally or physically attack those around them.

Often this is out of sheer frustration or irritation; instead of asking for help or taking the time to recognize why they are feeling these emotions, they resort to impulsive aggression to convey how they are feeling. But rather than intending to harm others, it's about lacking self-control before they take action. I've included strategies in the next section you can use to manage aggression and recognize the triggers or situations that contribute to your child's aggressive behavior.

ODD (Oppositional Defiance Disorder) and CD (Conduct Disorder) are common co-occurring conditions associated with half of the children diagnosed with ADHD. Both conduct disorders list aggression as a primary symptom. If your child seems to be suffering from the symptoms of either of these disorders, speak to your doctor or therapist, who can advise on the best plan of action and treatment.

- **Temper tantrums**

Preschoolers and toddlers are the main contenders for fantastic tantrum show-downs at home, school, and even the local supermarket. Ignoring these outbursts is often the best remedy as it teaches children that their negative behavior will not get them what they want and that there are better ways of expressing their needs. With time tantrums usually settle as children learn new coping skills and how to self-regulate.

Unfortunately, it's a little different for kids with ADHD, who are frequently overwhelmed by their feelings and emotions (emotional flooding). Putting their needs or wants on pause can be virtually impossible. As a direct result, they may often throw violent tantrums involving screaming, hitting, kicking, throwing themselves on the floor, and even biting. Consequently, the potential to hurt themselves and those around them, including you, is high.

For this reason, your child needs to understand that having ADHD isn't an excuse for tantrum throwing and poor behavior. Children with this condition also need to learn that certain actions have consequences, as this will help them flex their self-regulation 'muscles' and develop coping skills.

COPING STRATEGIES FOR DISRUPTIVE BEHAVIOUR

The coping strategies in the below section will help you navigate the emotional exhaustion felt by both you and your child due to disruptive behavior. As you incorporate the different activities into your life and routine, take the time to discover which strategies work best for your child.

Just because you have a child with ADHD doesn't mean they are a carbon copy of others with the same condition. What works well for your child may be ineffective for other kids. Your child is unique, a bespoke gift capable of a long and well-balanced, and fulfilling life because of their superhero parent – you. And, of course, the nifty strategies you're about to add to your arsenal against ADHD!

- **Lying**

ENCOURAGE HONESTY

The first step in the battle against lies is to encourage and emphasize the importance of honesty in everyday life. By this, I don't mean you should call your child out for every tall story because fanciful stories are part and parcel of a young child's development. Instead, use these tips to teach your child what can happen if they lie.

- Talk to your child about lying and telling the truth. Ask them how they would feel if someone told lies to them or what would happen if they lied to their teacher.
- Praise your child when they admit they have done something wrong. Rather than berating them, acknowledge and thank them for their honesty. Then, offer to help them resolve the issue.
- Be a truth ambassador yourself, own up when you get things wrong, and show your child that lies are not the answer to difficult situations.
- Avoid accusations as these can cause your child to feel there's no option but to lie to protect themselves from punishment. Instead, encourage your child to take ownership of their mistakes positively.

EXTINGUISHING DELIBERATE LIES

There are three steps to extinguishing the wildfire of deliberate lies.

1. Calm discussion

In a calm tone, explain how lies negatively impact relationships with family, friends, and teachers. Discuss what would happen if these people stopped trusting your child and how this would cause you to feel saddened and perhaps disappointed. This helps your child recognize the impact of dishonesty and how honesty is ultimately the best policy.

2. Acknowledge the lie

Always tell your child when you notice they are not being honest. However, avoid questioning their honesty constantly or accusing them of being a liar, as this will likely lead them to believe this is how you see them. As a result, they may not bother with telling the truth. Instead, mention you have noticed the lie and discuss why they felt the need to lie about the situation.

3. Eliminating the need to lie

Lying is often the result of stress or anxiety, the knee-jerk reaction most kids resort to when they feel trapped or battling with issues. Try to figure out why your child is telling lies. Is their homework too hard, and admitting they need help too embarrassing? Or perhaps they are lying to get things they want? In this case, a reward system could be an effective tool for allowing them to earn these things instead.

Past abuse and bullying can cause children to lie about serious issues because they fear punishment. If you believe your child is lying to protect someone, ensure your child understands they are safe when telling the truth and that you will try to help make things right.

TRUTH CHECK

If you suspect your child is lying, provide them with an opportunity to tell the truth. Tell them you will give them 10 minutes to reconsider their answer; let them know it's a truth check, and a different response isn't going to result in punishment. Then walk away and give them some time to consider whether they want to continue with the lie or admit to it. Kids with ADHD are prone to impulsive off-the-cuff answers when anxious or stressed; often, this is interpreted as dishonestly.

PREAMBLE METHOD

Setting the scene for honesty can be very helpful for children who feel pressured to be perfect or are anxious that telling the truth might affect their parent's approval. Instead, set the scene by mentioning you are about to ask a question that requires an honest answer. Then, state that you love them no matter their response and reiterate that sometimes mistakes happen and that dealing with errors positively is what matters. This provides your child a safe space to reflect and possibly tell the truth.

- **Defiance**

TURNING DEFIANCE INTO HEALTHY COMPLIANCE

Sometimes the words no and stop are enough to send a child with ODD or CD over the edge. Unfortunately, these standard discipline methods bounce off these conditions like rubber balls. Instead, positive reinforcement can encourage good behavior, and remaining calm when dealing with defiance can help soothe the situation.

Set expectations

House rules and behavior expectations should be clear and age appropriate. Ensure your child understands the consequences of breaking these rules and that there are no second chances for poor behavior. For example, refusing to complete their chores may have the consequence of losing their tv or screen time privileges for the day. Remember, while it may be hard enforcing consequences, it will prevent your child from ignoring you and undermining your authority.

Simplify Tasks

Complex tasks broken down into smaller, manageable chores prevent them from feeling overwhelmed and thus refusing to do them. For example, suppose they need to tidy their room; breaking the task down into individual actions such as making the bed, picking up the toys, and packing the books away can help them tackle the job effectively.

Encourage Frequent Exercise

Physical activity is highly beneficial for brain function and managing defiance and aggression in ADHD. Encourage your child to participate in sporting activities, dance, drama, or take them on a daily walk or bike ride. Playing the climbing frame at the park, hopscotch, and even a simple game of catch in the backyard can help with their feelings of frustration and being overwhelmed.

Don't Sweat The Small Things

Compromise is far better than full-blown war-fare. Instead, when your child exerts some control over a minor issue such as not wearing socks, come to an agreement that they should wear sturdier shoes when going out or slippers if at home. This allows you to remain firm in the face of bigger issues. Often children display defiant behavior when they want a say in how or when they should do things. Providing your child with choices helps them feel more in control. For example, instead of insisting chores are done at a specific time, request they are completed any time before dinner.

- **Too much screen time**

Although challenging, limiting and restricting screen time is essential as it helps your child develop a healthy approach to technology. In addition, instilling boundaries and balance can reduce the friction caused when it's time to turn off the device.

Schedule Screen Time

Have a set time that your child may use their tablet, phone, or watch tv. Children with ADHD tend to benefit from less screen time than their peers. However, rather than removing their device, help them use technology appropriately, monitor their usage, and teach them to recognize when it's time to put it down.

Ending screen time abruptly can also cause frustration; instead, warn your child that screen time is coming to an end soon. Provide this warning about ten minutes before the scheduled screen time is due to end, then five minutes before the end, ask them to confirm how much time is left. This helps them develop self-monitoring skills and self-control.

PARENTAL TOOLS & APPS

Parental apps that monitor usage and allow you to set timers are a great way to eliminate arguments when it's time to switch the screen off. Some apps allow parents to block certain websites or stop the internet connection to specific devices. Most internet providers offer these handy parental tools as a standard; alternatively, there are many free options online.

Implement screen-free zones & times

Implement screen-free zones (for the whole family) such as the dinner table, homework time, and just before bed. If the rule applies to the entire family, it won't seem like a punishment to your child.

Screen-free time also means better interaction between family members at dinner time and fewer distractions when completing school assignments. In addition, sleep health improves if devices are switched off at least 30-60 minutes before bedtime.

- **Food-related problems**

Eating a balanced and nutritious diet is beneficial for kids with ADHD. In chapter 5, we discussed the role of nutrition and elimination diets for kids with ADHD. While there is no substantial evidence to support that poor diet causes ADHD, it can negatively impact ADHD symptoms. This is because healthy brain function requires a good supply of nutrients, healthy fats, proteins, and carbohydrates.

I also mentioned the uncertainty around whether elimination diets actually worked. However, if you have discussed your child's dietary requirements with your doctor or nutritionist and you want to explore slowly eliminating or limiting certain foods, below is a list of foods you may want to consider.

◇ Sweets, Chocolate, Cake Frosting

Contain sugar, artificial colorants, and sweeteners which may impact ADHD symptoms.

◇ Soda, Sugary Milkshakes

Contain high levels of sugar, which can impact hyperactivity

◇ Coffee, Tea, Energy Drinks

Caffeine in tea, coffee, and energy drinks can contribute to hyperactivity and distractibility symptoms.

- **Whining**

Unfortunately, whining is a learned behavior, but it can be resolved by following these basic rules.

Step 1 – Stop the madness

Choose a quiet moment to discuss your child's whining with them. Explain that the new house rule is that you will stop listening and won't respond if they whine. The next time they whine, remain calm, keep your voice neutral and tell your child you can't understand them when they speak in that tone and when they talk nicely, you will listen.

Step 2 – Teach your child how to ask nicely

Some kids don't realize they are whining and may have no idea what it means. Use your phone to record your child when they are using a whiny tone and then when they are speaking in a pleasant voice. Play the recording back to them to illustrate what they sound like when whining and when talking nicely.

Step 3 – Praise, praise, praise

Too often, we as parents highlight negative behavior and then forget to praise our kids when they demonstrate good behavior. Positive reinforcement goes a long way to encouraging good behavior and reducing whining. The next time your child uses a pleasant tone when speaking to you, acknowledge their effort and thank them for speaking nicely.

Step 4 – Practice, practice, practice

Unlearning whiny behavior takes time; it won't happen overnight. Patience and consistency are crucial to eliminating the whiney communication skills your child has come to depend on.

- **Impulsive behavior**

Impulsive behavior needs to be replaced with appropriate behavioral patterns. These can be taught using simple strategies such as clarifying behavioral expectations, setting goals, and providing structure.

CLARIFY BEHAVIORAL EXPECTATIONS

New situations and environments can be overwhelming for a child with ADHD. Discuss upcoming events and explain the type of behavior required from them, what it looks and sounds like. For example, a visit to the doctor for a check-up requires quiet behavior because other patients might be unwell. Explain what will happen during the visit and how they should use their 'inside' voice, speak respectfully and sit quietly while waiting to be seen. During the activity, acknowledge your child's good behavior and reassure them they are behaving appropriately and doing well.

Use a reward system

Help your child set achievable impulse behavior goals and allow them to choose their reward or activity should they achieve it. This might be not saying hurtful things at the dinner table; if they manage to get through the meal without an outburst, they can reward themselves with an item or activity for meeting their goal. It's best to start small with impulse goals because they may lose interest if the goal is unachievable.

Plan the day

Structure can help to minimize impulsive behaviors. Unfortunately, kids with too much downtime are more likely to indulge in impulsive behaviors. Instead, set up a schedule that includes playtime, creative projects, exercise, homework, and chores. Allow your child to tick off each activity and move on to the next one. This provides them with a sense of control and achievement while ensuring they have less time for impulsivity.

- **Bedtime struggles**

Ensuring your child receives enough sleep is critical for development. Sufficient sleep also reduces irritability and other adverse sleep deprivation side effects that exacerbate ADHD symptoms.

Have a set bedtime routine

Routine and structure are important for kids with ADHD. While they may complain about getting ready for bed, following a routine of bathing, brushing teeth, reading, and having a set time for lights out is essential for providing a predictable and calming sleep environment. Keep the lights low for the hour before bedtime to help the body produce its natural sleep hormone – melatonin.

Set a bedtime alarm

Much like an alarm for waking up, the bedtime alarm is a quiet signal that it's time to rest. This removes the idea that parents are demanding they go to bed, and eventually, your child will associate this alarm with sleepiness.

Weighted blankets and blackout curtains

Blackout curtains can be used to keep the bedroom dark enough for melatonin production, promoting healthy sleep. In addition, kids with ADHD often struggle with poor proprioception (spatial awareness); the heavy pressure on their muscles and joints provided by a weighted blanket can help regulate and calm the body's senses and promote falling asleep naturally.

Melatonin Supplements

If your child isn't getting enough sleep, it may be that their body isn't producing enough melatonin. Speak to your doctor about your child taking a melatonin supplement and if it's the right option for their current treatment plan.

- **Aggression & Tantrums**

Sometimes, the smallest things trigger aggression in kids with ADHD. Impulsivity, changes in routine, and the misinterpretation of situations can all cause aggression and result in catastrophic tantrums in children with ADHD. Below are the dos and don'ts of managing the meltdowns.

Don't get angry – take deep breaths

Take at least ten breaths; this will help you lower your anxiety, calm your anger and allow you to think clearly. Teach your child to use the same technique when they start feeling upset.

Don't react – respond compassionately

If you and your child have an agreed plan for dealing with angry outbursts, now is the time to implement it. If not, you should discuss the problem and how you BOTH can work towards resolving it. Discuss your child's concerns and see if you can find a compromise that benefits both your needs and those of your child.

Don't dictate – discuss openly

When your child becomes agitated, ask them what is making them upset. Listen, and respond with empathy. Sometimes the reason for their agitation can quickly be resolved with a compromise; other times, they can't; learning to pick your battles is essential when dealing with ADHD. If it's one of those occasions when compromise is not possible, remind them to practice taking deep breaths to calm themselves.

Don't demand – remind and encourage

If your child is upset by your decision not to compromise, recognize their feelings and provide encouragement for calming down. Say things like – I know you are upset, but you are controlling your emotions really well. Kids with ADHD respond well to positive reinforcement rather than criticism. Gently remind them of your behavioral expectations and their own role in controlling their aggression.

Don't give up – remain committed and supportive

Raising children with ADHD requires patience and the quiet strength of a superhero at times! Join a support group for parents in similar situations; this will help you feel less alone in your war with ADHD. Finally, remember the progress you have made so far. Sometimes in the chaos of a meltdown, it can feel like you're losing the battle when in fact, the progress you and your child have made is nothing short of a miracle.

CODE WORDS

Using a code word as a signal for your child to calm down can help reduce emotional outbursts. Words such as no, stop, don't, etc., can trigger emotional responses in kids with ODD or CD. Your child can also use the same code word as a private signal to you that they are becoming upset. Allow your child to choose the code word; this could be something special to them, like the name of their favorite soccer team, color, or a funny, made-up word that may also diffuse the situation. My son's code word was and still is snap-crackle-pop, you guessed it, his favorite cereal!

Having strategies to cope with behavioral problems is much like having a war strategy in place. No self-respecting general would lead his troops into active battle without a solid plan in place. Not only does this ensure the safety of his men, but it also means he's guaranteed a triumphant victory. The same can be said for parents with kids that have ADHD; as they implement effective behavioral strategies, they too can be victorious in the face of ADHD.

9

SOME LESSONS IN MANNERS

"Your mood should not dictate your manners."

— ANONYMOUS

Can you imagine a world without manners? When my son was still relatively young, I remember sitting at the dinner table calmly chatting about the day when, to my horror, he reached across my plate to grab an extra bread roll. When I mentioned my displeasure with his actions, he mumbled, his mouth full of bread, that I hadn't heard he wanted another one when he asked for it. Needless to say, we had a gentle chat about table manners and how one should wait to ask for extra food politely.

My first thought was, thank goodness there were no guests at the table. I would have been mortified at his actions. It's not like we hadn't taught him basic table manners; he just needed reminding at times, which I'm sure is true for many young children. However, if we had left his poor table behavior to continue into adulthood, it would have made for some very embarrassing dinner dates! However, manners are more than showing good etiquette at the dinner table.

When we were young, our parents taught us to say please and thank you, reminded us to be respectful to our elders, and requested that we shake hands when meeting people. It's these little social 'norms' that make life pleasant and ensure our interactions with others are polite and civilized. Furthermore, they directly impact our communication and relationships with others, both of which are integral to becoming successful adults.

As parents, whether our children have ADHD or not, it's our job to ensure that our kids are well-mannered, as this provides the foundation for well-rounded and successful adults.

IMPORTANCE OF GOOD MANNERS

While some parents may feel that teaching their child manners is a little outdated in today's modern society, the truth is without manners, civilized society as we know it wouldn't exist. A broad definition of civilized society is an ordered way of life with reasonable laws and customs that treats everyone fairly and indiscriminately. This ultimately boils down to showing respect to others. Respect is important for keeping the peace, reducing disputes, and living in harmony with others.

If you think your child's manners don't affect society, think about this. All children eventually become adults, and it's these adults that will become the next generation of parents. If they have no idea how to treat others respectfully, how will they teach their own children?

Moreover, without good manners, civilized society is at risk of disintegrating into violence and chaos. Not that I'm suggesting a child without manners will lead to an apocalypse, but it can have some pretty catastrophic effects on their development and personality. Without manners, your child may be seen as selfish and unkind; this can impact their ability to interact with others socially and prevent them from developing professional connections in the workplace.

WHY TEACHING GOOD MANNERS TO KIDS IS ESSENTIAL

- **Manners show respect**

All people are deserving of respect and consideration. Teaching our children to consider others is more than simply teaching them to say please and thank you. It's about teaching them to recognize that everyone around them has 'value' and that the way they are treated is extremely important.

Teach your child to treat others in the same way that they would like to be treated. This provides them with a good yardstick to use when showing care for others. After all, as humans, we naturally don't like to be treated badly, so if we don't want the same treatment, we shouldn't do it either.

- **They form the foundation of healthy relationships**

Respect and consideration are the cornerstones of strong, healthy friendships, relationships, and social connections. When children have good manners, those they communicate with respond well and respond similarly. This is what I call the manners-mirror effect.

Teach your child that how they project themselves to others will directly influence how others project back to them. Therefore, if they are rude, they should expect rudeness in return and so on.

- **Manners Build confidence**

Good manners promote positive interactions with others. This makes your child feel good about themselves and builds their confidence. In addition, when your child has good manners, their social and communication skills become stronger.

Teaching Good Manners

My son and I used to love playing a copycat game we made up. I would walk ahead of him, and he would copy my movements. Of course, I would make all sorts of funny gestures, movements, and sounds, and he would laugh and follow by doing exactly the same thing. Looking back, I realize he was mimicking me all the time, not just when we played our special game. From the way I stirred my tea to the way I spoke on my phone or tidied the toys away, he seemed to be my mini carbon copy.

It's like this for most kids; they are sponges absorbing information from their surroundings by watching and following closely. It's quite a sobering thought to realize that the way we act and interact with others is mimicked and followed closely by our children.

Of course, parents make mistakes, we're only human, but if our kids constantly see poor behavior and manners emanating from us, it makes sense that they will feel this is the correct way to behave. Therefore, as parents, we need to be hyper-aware that our kids naturally see us as role models, making it imperative that the behavior we model to them is worthy of copying.

TIPS & STRATEGIES FOR GOOD ROLE MODEL BEHAVIOR

- **Be an encourager**

Encourage your child to do their best and recognize their efforts to achieve their goals in a positive way. Unrealistic expectations can place a lot of stress and pressure on your child. Instead, celebrate their uniqueness and the great qualities they possess.

- **Be supportive and a good listener**

Become a good listener. Set aside time each day dedicated to listening to your child and what they have to share with you. When our kids feel comfortable speaking to us, they open up and provide opportunities for us to provide the support and help they need.

This could be a chat about how their day went at school or catch-up after dinner on a topic of their choice. Sometimes we are so busy 'teaching' our kids that we forget to 'listen' – they have some amazing things to share if we let them.

- **Don't blow things out of proportion**

Remember to remain balanced and resist going overboard in your attempts to be the perfect role model. Heaping unrealistic amounts of praise on your child can leave them feeling uncomfortable and awkward.

- **Be the best version of you**

As parents, we have significant influence over our children. They look to us for inspiration and guidance; therefore, our words and actions are extremely important as they may influence and impact their interactions with others. Take a moment to consider your words, actions, and reactions before you verbalize or demonstrate them in front of your child.

- **Be mindful of tone and body language**

Don't shout or demonstrate aggressive or threatening body language when speaking to your child. Instead, moderate your tone, resist using hurtful or negative language and keep your request simple and direct. Rather than losing control of your emotions, keep your cool and burn off the frustration with exercise.

- **Be open and honest**

Let your child get to know the real you. While you may want to be the perfect role model, the fact is, role models also have their weaknesses. Admit to your mistakes and chat openly to your child about them so they can learn from your experience. A positive attitude to ward setbacks and failures in your own life will teach your child that making mistakes is human; it's how you 'bounce back' from them that matters.

- **Walk the talk; don't just talk the talk**

Dictating expected behaviors from your child that are not emulated by you will soon result in open revolt! Instead, your words should match your actions, and this can only be done by actively showing your child that you abide by your own code of conduct.

- **Teach your kids to be respectful**

Teaching respect means showing respect in the first instance. This means as parents, we should show respect to our children by valuing their opinions and thoughts. Model respect in front of your kids, and be respectful when interacting with others, and your child will start to do the same.

- **Discuss bullying and why it's never okay**

Teach your child to be respectful, kind, and considerate of others. Encouraging your child to consider how others are feeling will teach them to be empathetic and can ensure your child doesn't engage in bullying behaviors.

WHAT NOT TO DO

Sometimes without realizing it, we parents model negative behaviors in front of our children. Below are some examples of how unhealthy behaviors unwittingly creep into our lives and affect our child's behavior.

- **Don't lie**

John tells the ticket booth office at the amusement park that his 12-year-old daughter is only 11, so he can get a cheaper entrance ticket. She learns it's okay to lie to get what you want.

- **Don't be disrespectful**

Suzie expects her son to treat everyone with respect but frequently makes negative comments about her friends behind their backs.

- **Don't dictate**

Mary tells her children they need to make healthy food choices but often eats desserts and chocolates after they have gone to bed.

- **Don't be unkind**

Jack tells his son to be kind to others but shouts at the waitress when she makes a mistake with their food order.

- **Don't go against your own advice**

Lara is frequently told by her parents that she needs to read more but has heard them tell their friends they don't enjoy reading books.

- **Don't display poor leadership skills**

Sam tells his children to be generous and share what they have with others but never volunteers for charity or makes donations.

In summary, instilling good behavior, etiquette and manners don't require a dictatorship; instead, they require a true role model who is willing to lead by example.

WHEN YOUR KIDS WON'T LISTEN

It can be quite humiliating and frustrating when your child doesn't listen to you. As you watch them running through the store, crashing into people, or bouncing like a wild Mexican bean on a friend's sofa, it can be tempting to yell and scream your lungs out in fury. And no one understands this feeling more than me. However, while it's completely understandable to feel angry, venting your anger by yelling isn't going to provide a positive solution.

WHY DON'T KIDS LISTEN?

Listening is a two-way street; as much as you talk to your child, you should be providing them with an equal opportunity to speak to you.

Encouraging good listening skills begins with us, the parents, modeling good communication and actively listening to our kids. Taking the time to consider their concerns and worries shows you respect them and makes it easier for them to show respect to you.

It's also important to remember that not listening isn't always a sign of disrespect. Issues such as hearing loss, mental health disorders, and auditory processing issues can contribute to your child not listening or paying attention.

Kids with ADHD often struggle with inattentiveness and hyperactivity, making it more difficult for them to focus and follow instructions or process what you are saying. Sometimes your message may be too long or too complex for them to decipher; as a result, it's easier to ignore what you are saying because it's just too difficult and frustrating for them to follow.

TIPS TO ENCOURAGE KIDS TO LISTEN

Teaching your child healthy listening skills takes patience and consistency.

- **Make Eye Contact**

When speaking to your child, ensure your instructions aren't being bellowed from downstairs or from the other room. This simply provides the opportunity to ignore your requests. Instead, when entering the room to speak to your child, gently touch their arm or shoulder to gain their attention and make eye contact when speaking to them. This ensures they are focusing on you and strengthens communication.

- **Communicate, don't argue**

Effective communication is about getting the timing right. Consider the timing of your request; if your child is in the middle of a game or an activity, expecting them to immediately stop and listen to you may be less effective than if you gave them a heads up that you wanted to talk in a few minutes. Making space to talk without distraction will ensure they focus on your message and hear what you are saying.

Of course, if they refuse to listen, it can be tempting to get sucked into arguing with your child. However, don't allow your emotions to take over, remain neutral, and speak clearly and calmly.

- **Advise, don't make speeches**

Keep your message short, concise, and clear. Inattentiveness associated with ADHD can make following long messages tricky. As a result, long speeches may mean your child automatically stops listening and tunes you out!

- **Set realistic expectations**

Ensure your child understands what you are asking of them. Of course, your expectations should be realistic and appropriate for your child's age and developmental stage.

In terms of behavior, discuss what this looks like and how it sounds. Offer advice about how they can achieve this behavior and how you can help. Then discuss the consequences of poor behavior ahead of time. These should be reasonable and logical such as going home or an allotted time-out period.

- **Ensure comprehension**

Once you have delivered your message, ask your child to repeat back to you what they understood from your request. This ensures your child has heard and understood the instructions and improves communication and cooperation. If they haven't understood what is required of them, this is their opportunity to ask questions and for you to clarify any ambiguity.

- **Offer choices**

When asking your child to do something, offer them a choice as this takes away the frustration of following yet another 'order' and allows them to feel they have an input in their lives. For example, rather than saying do your homework, ask them what assignment they would like to start with, math or science.

Having a choice also helps kids with ADHD flex their executive function muscles as they learn good decision-making skills.

- **Be consistent**

Mixed messages are a recipe for disaster. Your instructions and behavioral expectations should remain consistent, so your child knows what is expected of them and doesn't become confused.

- **Reward good behavior**

Always remember to praise good behavior and, in particular, good listening skills. If your child listens to you without complaining, use little rewards or incentives to further encourage good listening behaviors. This is called positive reinforcement. For example, you ask your child to stop playing their computer game and join the family for dinner. If they come to dinner without complaining, you could allow them to play their game for an extra fifteen minutes after dinner.

ACTIVITIES THAT TEACH GOOD VALUES

Developing your child's moral compass doesn't have to be boring and filled with constant lecturing. Take a look at some of the interactive activities you can use to teach your child good values.

- **Reading and telling stories**

Most children's stories focus on teaching a valuable life lesson. Choose stories that focus on good values, manners, and appropriate behavior to support the lessons you are trying to teach your kids.

A good example of this is Aesop's Fables which are short stories that illustrate the impact of kindness, compassion, lies, and honesty.

- **Singing**

Young children love to sing, especially if the song is silly and the tune is catchy. The internet is full of cute songs that teach youngsters good values. My personal favorite is the manners song I taught my son. We used to sing this song on the way to school in the hopes it would set the tone for good behavior for the day!

Manners:
(sung to the tune of twinkle star)

"We say, "Thank you." We say, "Please."
We don't interrupt or tease.
We don't argue. We don't fuss-
Listen when folks talk to us
We share things and take our turn.
Manners are so easy to learn.

— AUTHOR UNKNOWN

Encourage older children to listen to music that has positive and inspirational messages about life in their lyrics.

- **Games**

Games are also an interactive way of teaching our children values. When playing games, children develop social skills and learn valuable life lessons. These include learning to lose graciously, teamwork, waiting their turn (respect for others), and accepting victory humbly.

- **Plant a tree/ go litter picking**

Teaching our kids to care about more than their immediate surroundings allows them to feel as though they are actively contributing to their community. It gives them a sense of purpose and teaches them to have social responsibility.

Preparing our kids for adult life is one of our most important jobs as parents. Equipping them with good manners and the necessary values will help them become decent members of society. As a result, their communications with others will be respectful and empathetic, which in turn will help them forge strong social and professional relationships.

10

HELL, DON'T YELL!

"Anger Is Never Without A Reason, But Seldom A Good One."

— BENJAMIN FRANKLIN

I could feel the heat creeping up my neck, over my jawline, and into my face. The muscle in my jaw ached as I clenched my teeth and desperately tried to hold onto my temper. Sucking air in through my nose, it refused to come out of my mouth as the 'calming' breathing exercises advised. Instead, it remained painfully trapped in my chest, which was threatening to explode. Finally, before my tongue had the chance to spew forth the angry tirade it was desperate to vocalize, I made the conscious decision to leave the room.

My anger at the time seemed justified; after all, how many times is a parent expected to say the same thing? Of course, reminding my son about things wasn't the problem; it was the defiance and backchat I had to endure as payment for my 'good parenting' efforts.

Usually, the above scenario would have ended in me shouting and yelling to get my point across or force my son into some form of action. Not that this technique ever worked, which left me feeling even more frustrated and angry. I didn't realize that this vicious circle of poor communication was equally frustrating to my child and further fuelled his angry outbursts towards me. That saying 'you reap what you sow' is very true when it comes to emotions, especially anger. The more anger I showed towards my son, the more he reflected back toward me.

It took stepping back from the situation for me to realize that my parenting techniques may be the cause of the friction in our home. This was a difficult pill to swallow, especially since I was trying my best to be the supportive parent my son needed. However, putting my pride aside, I decided to do some research and found to my embarrassment, there were quite a few issues with my parenting style, most of which I had been unaware of until then!

PARENTING PITFALLS

Unfortunately, being a parent doesn't automatically mean we don't make mistakes; it's what makes us human. And although we strive to be the superheroes in our children's lives, even superheroes make mistakes; look at superman's unfortunate wardrobe error! However, underpants aside, the pitfalls we accidentally slip into can significantly impact our parenting abilities.

- **Ignoring problems**

Sometimes it's easier to assume the ostrich stance and stick our heads in the sand than admit we need help. As a result, parents struggle for years with issues that could quickly be resolved with some help and advice. Parents can use the internet, books, and forums to research and discuss parenting issues ranging from behavioral problems to tantrums and sleep troubles. Alternatively, have a friendly chat with your pediatrician or health care provider if you have any doubts.

- **Misunderstanding problems**

When identifying problems, you need to assess what is or isn't a problem. Some things may seem like a big problem but are part and parcel of normal development.

For example, is it a 'big' problem if:

a) Your teen starts to test the boundaries a bit more and comes home 10 minutes late from a party
b) Your six-year-old becomes curious about their sexuality
c) Your preschooler sometimes throws a tantrum

The above are age-appropriate developmental stages in children and are not significant issues. However, your teen staying out all night or stealing are big issues.

- **Having unrealistic expectations**

Each child develops at their own pace. Just because your neighbor's child was potty trained at 20 months doesn't mean your 2 ½-year-old who isn't interested in this process yet has a problem. Match your expectations to your child's capabilities and developmental maturity.

Sometimes our expectations are on target, but we add that dreaded ingredient called perfection. Of course, we want our children to excel, but expecting them to be perfect can negatively impact their self-esteem and cause self-confidence issues. On the other hand, setting realistic expectations allows our children to face setbacks positively and inspires them to succeed when trying again.

- **Being inconsistent**

Inconsistent parenting is like driving a car with a fluctuating gas pedal. Either you put your foot too hard on the gas, don't use the gas at all, or apply a slight pressure that isn't enough to move the car forward at all. Remember those learning to drive days? The same happens when we are inconsistent with our parenting style. For example, you may decide to be strict today and give in to things tomorrow. Unfortunately, this approach causes confusion as your child struggles to know what is expected of them.

- **Not setting limits**

All children benefit from limits, rules, and routines. Having a boundary in which to work provides security and helps your child understand what is expected of them.

You may want your child to make their own decisions, but ultimately, they need to recognize your authority. Allowing the house rules to be negotiated and changed too often can cause power struggles between you and your kid.

- **Fighting back**

I'm not talking about physical conflict but rather the fighting, yelling, and endless repetition that occurs when we get stuck in the vortex of arguing with our kids. Arguing provides your child with negative attention and power over you and your reactions.

It also rewards bad behavior. The only way to stop this endless circle is to STOP.

Stop yelling, stop repeating and start using other techniques such as time out and logical consequences for misbehavior. Lastly, don't waste any time arguing before implementing them!

- **Not changing what isn't working**

Consequences are a way of teaching our children not to indulge in bad behavior. If they don't achieve this, then they are ineffective discipline techniques. Unfortunately, what works for one kid doesn't always work for another. For example, you may use time-out as a consequence for tantrums, but if your child continues to throw tantrums every day despite regular time-outs, it's time to change the game plan!

- **Making empty threats**

Sometimes in desperation, we can find ourselves threatening our kids with dire consequences in an attempt to get them to listen. Unfortunately, if we don't follow through with the threat, our kids eventually realize that we don't 'mean' what we say, so the bad behavior continues. Instead, keep consequences realistic and ensure you implement them consistently.

- **Relying too much on older parenting tactics**

Our parents did it, their parents did it, and their parents before them did it. What did they do? They trusted their gut instincts regarding parenting and hoped for the best. Unfortunately, life isn't the same as back then; the world is faster, technology has taken over, and today's kids develop at a rate that leaves us reeling.

However, it also means that today's parents can access more help and support than was previously around. As a result, childhood issues and parenting mistakes are identified sooner and resolved. Remember, just because your parents used tactics that 'seemed' to work doesn't mean they are appropriate for your child. As parents, we have access to so much information and advice; it might be time to revamp our parenting tactics wardrobe!

- **Forgetting the joy of childhood**

Sometimes we get so caught up with the issues that arise when raising kids with ADHD that we forget they're only kids. Childhood should be a magical adventure filled with exciting experiences and fun. Your child is unique and wonderfully made; remember to appreciate and celebrate their abilities, achievements, and specialness.

YELLING IS NOT A SOLUTION

Once you have identified the pitfalls that apply to your parenting style, it's time to get a 'handle' on the anger and eradicate yelling from your communication. This is possibly the hardest step when developing a better relationship with our children. Because they have a secret weapon, they know exactly which buttons to press to trigger a reaction! But we can regain control of the situation by learning to manage our anger.

ANGER MANAGEMENT TIPS FOR PARENTS

- **Identify your trigger points**

Everyone's trigger points are different. It may be how your child backchats or doesn't listen; it could even be a messy room; whatever the reason for your anger, it's important to identify how you feel when you start to get angry. These are the warning signs that help you recognize your anger so you can begin to work on calming yourself down. For example, you may notice you clench your teeth or hands; your heart rate speeds up, or you start to feel hot and bothered (hands up, Lina Cole!)

- **Find a safe space to process and listen to your thoughts**

Once you have recognized the early warning signs of your anger, you can start working on calming down. First, ask someone to watch your child (if they are too young to be on their own) and go somewhere quiet, such as the park, garden, or even the bathroom. The important thing here is to put some space between you and your child.

Negative thought patterns can also increase anger. Check in with your thoughts and ensure you aren't adding to your anger by thinking things like:

- ◇ Why can't they behave better?
- ◇ I have to do everything; no one ever helps me
- ◇ No one listens to me
- ◇ My kids are so naughty

Try to play devil's advocate with yourself and provide a positive answer for each negative thought. For example, remembering how your kids behaved well yesterday or how they helped tidy up without being asked this morning goes a long way to calming the negative statements you may use to criticize yourself.

- **Observe your body**

Notice how your body is physically reacting to your anger. Below are some of the common physical signs brought on by anger.

- Sweating
- Fast heart rate
- Hyperventilating
- Tense muscles in the neck and shoulders
- Facial flushing
- Clenched teeth/hands
- Agitation
- Churning stomach

- **Try to calm down**

Slow your breathing as this will slow your heart rate down. To do this, breathe in through your nose for two seconds and out through your mouth for four seconds. Keep doing this until your heart rate settles back into a normal rhythm.

If you can't leave your child and they are yelling or screaming, use noise-canceling headphones or earphones to reduce the noise. Sometimes simply blocking your ears with your fingers is the fastest solution! Keep taking slow, deep breaths.

Practice self-soothing; this technique isn't only for babies and children; as adults, we need to know how to self-soothe to reduce stress. Do something you enjoy, such as listening to music, talking to a friend about the situation, or going for a walk.

- **Reflect on the situation & ask the right questions**

Once you have calmed down, go over what happened and try to learn from the experience. Then, ask yourself the following questions:

◇ Why did I get so upset?
◇ Was my anger proportional to my child's actions/words?
◇ How can I positively resolve the issue?
◇ Do I need to ask for help or do something about this?
◇ How do we (my child and I) move forward from here?

When our children are difficult, it's often easier to let our tempers flare than to stop and realize there may be something else behind their misbehavior. I'm not playing the blame game here; I'm guilty of this too. Being too tired, stressed, or busy can easily impact our tolerance levels.

Ask yourself one final question: Why is my child behaving this way? Often children act out for a reason. Hunger, boredom, tiredness, and even attention seeking are common reasons kids act out. Try to meet your child's needs rather than letting your anger get the best of you.

- **Keep an anger journal**

Keeping a journal that records how and when you get angry will help you pinpoint patterns or triggers that spark your anger. Use this information to strategize and implement plans to alleviate these anger-fueled sessions. Chat to your kids about the things that get you angry and ask them to help you find ways to improve the friction. Making them part of the solution is often the best approach!

- **Minimize marriage spats**

Arguing in front of your child can cause significant anxiety and stress. Instead, strategize with your spouse about how to handle these situations. For example, you and your spouse could have a code word that signals you are too angry to discuss the situation now and need time to cool off first. Alternatively, you could agree that either of you can walk away during a discussion if you become angry in front of the kids.

FORGING BETTER RELATIONSHIPS

Sometimes our relationships with our kids break down to such a point they need repairing. However, regaining trust on both sides takes time and patience, and no matter how much we wish things would fix themselves overnight, good relationships take hard work and a lot of effort on both sides.

- **Focus on the issues rather than dishing out blame**

Identify the issues and focus on resolving them without pointing fingers and engaging in personal attacks.

- **Ease back into the relationship**

Regaining a good relationship with your child will take time. Instead of rushing in, take the relationship slowly, at a pace that is comfortable for both you and your child.

- **Look after yourself, too**

So often, parents forget to practice self-care. Life becomes too busy; demanding schedules, parenting responsibilities, and hectic social lives usually mean that we are left tired, drained, and stressed. This doesn't bode well for good parenting techniques or managing anger and stress. Set time aside for you where you can relax and regroup away from the situation.

Ask a friend/family member to watch your child for the evening/weekend and plan some 'me' time. This could include:

- ◇ Going to watch a movie
- ◇ Getting a haircut/manicure/pedicure
- ◇ Having lunch with a friend
- ◇ Booking a spa day

- **Set new boundaries**

Establish what you want from this new relationship with your child. Then, discuss this openly with them and decide what a healthy relationship looks like for both of you.

It's important to note that the previous boundaries (if any) were not working, so new ones need to be implemented. For example, when you say 'no,' you mean 'no,' and consequences for bad behavior once agreed upon are going to be consistently applied.

- **Beware of your limits**

Set reasonable expectations for yourself, you are only human, and everyone has their limit regarding what they can deal with or handle appropriately. You may find yourself exhausted and stressed when you get home from work. As a result, this time of day may not be the best to approach difficult conversations or issues. Instead, wait until you have destressed with a cup of tea or have been for a walk or run.

- **Learn to let go**

Instead of focusing on how annoyed you are with your child, focus on the issue that needs resolving. It's too easy to become entangled in an emotional slanging match when having a calm conversation with your child about the problem is more beneficial. Allow your child to express their opinion and listen to them but be assertive with your expectations and views as well.

Using 'I' statements rather than 'you' statements is also less antagonistic and goes a long way to keeping tensions to a minimum. For example, instead of saying, 'you didn't do your chores,' you could say, 'I get frustrated when you don't do your chores on time.'

Lastly, remember to forgive yourself. Getting angry is a normal human response to stressful situations. While this doesn't make it okay to yell at your kids, it does mean that sometimes even superheroes need to count to ten!

TEACHING EMPATHY TO YOUR KIDS

Kids with ADHD struggle with empathy, not because they are uncaring by any means but because their inattentiveness and distraction can come across as insensitive or self-absorbed. Often this is the very reason why we parents become frustrated and yell! However, there are ways to teach our children to be empathetic.

- **Be a role model**

Children are masters of the old copycat game; if you show them how to behave, the results are much better than simply dictating. Likewise, when we show others sympathy, respect, or celebrate their achievements, our kids are watching and will start to emulate us.

- **Celebrate the success of everyone**

Sometimes parents hesitate to celebrate the achievements of friends or siblings in case the child with

ADHD feels bad. However, on the flip side, if the child with ADHD is the only one receiving praise, they learn that their achievements matter above those of others.

- **Talk about & label feelings**

Be open about feelings and emotions and discuss them with your child regularly. Talk about the things that make them happy, excited, sad, or angry. Once they have learned to identify their own feelings, play 'spot the emotion game' each time you go out.

The game is simple; all your child has to do is identify how they think other people are feeling. For example, they may see a child drop their ice cream at the beach; in that case, if they recognize the child may be feeling sad, they score a point. However, if the chosen emotion is wrong, it's an opportunity for you to explain the difference between the emotion they chose and the correct one.

- **Teach them to handle adversity positively**

Disappointments and setbacks can cause children to feel negative emotions such as anger or jealousy. However, teaching our children to handle these emotions positively increases emotional intelligence and strengthens empathy.

- **Explain individuality and uniqueness**

Teach your child to accept everyone's culture, faith, belief, and lifestyle. Teaching our children to be tolerant of differences and see situations from another's perspective increases empathy.

- **Point out similarities**

Explain that although each person is different on the outside, we all experience similar emotions such as sadness, anger, and happiness.

- **Practice emotional facial expressions**

Smiling triggers happiness even if you don't feel happy at that point in time. Try it; it works! In fact, it's thought that often an empathetic response occurs if our facial expression matches the feelings of the other person. For example, if someone is sad and you make a sad face, you will experience empathy. Use TV or books to identify emotions in others, then ask your child to make a facial expression to match this and describe how they are feeling.

I'm not going to sugar-coat the truth; parenting is tough and parenting a child with ADHD is even more challenging. However, it can also be extremely rewarding when using disciplining strategies that work rather than yelling or aggression.

11

COLLABORATING WITH SCHOOLS

"Alone We Can Do So Little; Together We Can Do So Much."

— HELEN KELLER

I've always thought parenting is one of the most challenging professions. Unlike company CEO and director job roles, the role of being a parent isn't supported by years of training and management courses. Instead, we're thrown into the proverbial deep end without even a courtesy interview process!

Our parenting journey begins with a stressful 9-ish months filled with anxiety about the non-existent parenting skills we have and worrying if 'this' was a huge mistake. At least that's how I felt sitting on the edge of the hospital bed while in labor with my son and wondering if somehow, I could reverse time. I felt so unprepared.

Let's be honest, most of us enter parenthood blinded by a false sense of security, believing that natural instinct will automatically kick in and that somehow the birthing process will make us veritable gurus on all things child related. That is until day one, when this tiny, helpless creature first enters our lives, takes over our hearts, and leaves us quaking in fear as we realize how little we know about raising a child.

Of course, we instinctively love them and want to protect them, but, unfortunately, this also means we somehow tap into this belief that we must do this all on our own. If only kids came with a bespoke 'how to' manual – it would save a lot of issues!

The belief we need to parent alone sort of works until they reach preschool age, when suddenly the specter of ADHD looms, introduced to us one Friday afternoon by a tired teacher who's seen it all before. If only her suspicions had been wrong!

We just thought our kids were a little 'boisterous' or 'disinterested' now it turns out they have a condition, which, you guessed it, we have no idea how to handle. Unfortunately, unlike those company tycoons I mentioned, there isn't an emergency meeting available, presentation, or email advising on the best course of action. Instead, we parent of kids with ADHD find ourselves wading through a quagmire of self-help research and information as we try to familiarize ourselves with this chronic condition.

However, the good news is, unlike our preconceived notions of parenthood, parenting does not have to be a lonely journey – even if your child has ADHD. That saying 'it takes a village to raise a child' is very true. With the help and support of family, friends, and professionals, we can give our kids a fantastic start to adult life, and it all begins with the collaboration of parents and educators.

ROLE OF SCHOOLS

How ADHD affects kids at school

The primary symptoms of ADHD are hyperactivity and inattentiveness. These symptoms can affect your child's ability to listen, sit still and focus in the classroom leading to poor performance. Common issues kids with ADHD struggle with in the classroom include:

- Paying attention and ignoring distractions
- Starting or finishing assignments
- Remaining seated/working quietly
- Staying organized

In addition, co-occurring learning disabilities can also cause challenges in the classroom environment.

HOW CAN TEACHERS HELP KIDS WITH ADHD?

Teachers play a vital role in the development and progress of all children in their care. When they understand a child's learning requirements, they can use various tools to assist with their education. The IEP (Individual Education Program) and the 504 plan are examples of this type of assistance. They can help tailor bespoke educational strategies and related services or changes to the classroom environment to address your child's academic needs.

Teachers can help assess whether your child would benefit from an IEP or 504 plan.

▷ **504 Plan**

Section 504 of the US Rehabilitation Act of 1973 ensures kids in public schools or publically funded private schools receive fair treatment based on their physical and mental disabilities. This ensures the academic challenges they face are considered while in education.

Who qualifies for a 504 plan, and how does it work?

Students who have disabilities that affect the below abilities qualify for a 504 plan:

- The ability to communicate (speak/hear/see)
- The ability to move (stand/bend/lift/work)
- Basic functional issues (breathe/sleep/eat/walk)
- Focus and attention issues (read/think/learn/concentrate)

The primary purpose of a 504 plan is to educate kids with ADHD in regular classrooms while providing the support, services, or education aids they require. This might require changes to how the classroom is run and how your child is supported.

Below are some of the ways a 504 plan can help your child.

- Seating plans (away from noise/distraction)
- Visual/verbal aids (including technology)
- Audio- video materials
- Modified books and learning materials

- Adjusted classwork/class schedules/grading techniques
- Verbal assessment instead of written tests
- Support with behavior management
- Extra time provided for assessments/assignments
- Leniency for missing work and being late or absent

504 plans are created by a team usually consisting of the principal, parents, and teachers. Other school personnel such as the school guidance counselor and the school nurse should also form part of the team. These plans are reviewed annually to ensure they continue to meet the child's needs or implement further changes if necessary. If you feel your child would benefit from a 504 plan, chat to your school representative about your school's evaluation and referral process.

▷ **IEP**

An IEP (Individualized Education Program) is free to parents with kids in public schools. This specialized education service provides extra help and support for kids with conditions that affect their learning abilities. Below are some of the eligibility criteria for an IEP plan.

- ADHD/Autism
- Mental illness (depression/anxiety)
- Cognitive impairments
- Developmental issues/delays
- Physical disability
- Hearing impairments
- Vision impairments
- Speech/language issues
- Learning disabilities

Professionals who help develop the IEP plan include teachers, therapists (physical, speech, occupational), and a psychologist depending on your child's needs.

An IEP program provides additional support services such as counseling, speech therapy, and special education. These plans are reviewed annually but can be done sooner if the child's educational needs change.

What are the differences between a 504 and IEP plan?

504 Plan	IEP Program
Regular classroom setting	Regular or specialized setting
Monitored by the classroom teacher	Monitored by the classroom teacher and additional support staff
Modifies regular teaching programs	Additional/different educational services based on student needs
No parent permission/involvement required	Parent permission and involvement required

Children with an IEP also benefit from the services and protections a 504 plan provides. This means a child with ADHD could have both an IEP and 504 plan (combined) to give them the best support and protection in educational settings.

Teachers can provide regular progress reports.

Regular updates between you and your child's teacher can help monitor and track their progress. Furthermore, if additional support is required, it can be implemented quickly using the right services. For example, a folder or small diary can be used to communicate notes and daily progress between home and school.

Teachers can help your child achieve their academic goals

All teachers want their students to succeed. When they understand a student's challenges, such as with ADHD, their input can positively affect your child's output in terms of academic success. For example, they could do things like:

- Provide praise for efforts
- Be positive and encouraging
- Minimize distractions in the classroom by rearranging seating plans
- Assist with remaining organized
- Remind kids to stay focused on tasks
- Provide adequate breaks for movement
- Allow extra time to complete assignments and class work
- Provide simple, clear instructions
- Break tasks down into manageable steps
- Teach kids to slow down, check work, and correct mistakes
- Teach study skills (reading aloud, test preparation, taking notes)
- Have structure in the classroom (rules and routines)
- Provide choices for completing assignments (verbal, written, project building)

HOW CAN PARENTS COLLABORATE WITH TEACHERS TO HELP KIDS?

Many parents leave the job of educating their kids to their teachers, but the truth is that for education to be successful, it requires the input of both parent and teacher. In fact, I would go so far as to say it's crucial for the successful education of kids with ADHD. Parents can work with teachers in several ways to ensure their child's education remains on track and help them manage their school day.

Have regular monthly meetings with your child's teacher or school counselor to discuss their needs and progress. It's also an excellent time to discuss any issues or set goals that need to be achieved.

Of course, it can be hard to hear negative things about your child's behavior or learning approach, but remember these meetings are so you can understand your child's education challenges and help them manage them.

Share relevant information about your child's struggles at home or socially; this will give educators a better understanding of the issues your child is facing. In addition, advise them of any behavioral tips or techniques that work well and provide information regarding medications and other treatments.

TIPS FOR MAKING LEARNING FUN

We all learn better when we are having fun, and this is especially true for kids with ADHD. The results are exponentially better when information is provided in a fun, interactive way that is easy to understand and process. Identifying how your child learns best can help them absorb the necessary information.

- **Visual Learners**

Reading and visual cues are best for this type of student. They learn well using drawings, flashcards, and written information. Brightly colored sticky notes and vision boards are excellent tools to assist with their studies.

- **Auditory Learners**

Learning by talking and listening is easier for this learner. In addition, verbal tests and assessments are more beneficial for auditory learners.

- **Tactile Learners**

Tactile learners do better when lessons include physical touch or movement. For example, using counters (jelly beans) for math lessons or dress-up costumes for acting out poetry and other lesson facts.

Once you have assessed how your child enjoys learning, you can use many fun interactive ways to help them view learning positively.

Sing it or Say it – make up funny acronyms, songs, or phrases to help them remember the order of math operations or spellings.

Draw it – illustrations are easier to understand than the spoken or written word. For example, a math problem involving ten cars is much easier to understand if there is a visual aid to support it.

Play it – dominoes, dice, counters, and memory cards are all fun ways of solving math problems. Alternatively, take off your shoes and use your fingers and toes to find the correct answer!

Dramatize it – Act out stories and allow your child to join in; use funny voices and impromptu costumes (tea towels/ tablecloths) to bring characters to life.

Place your bets! – Engage your child in assessing what will happen next in the story. For example, you might say, "The boy in the story seems very happy– I bet he's going to play in the park with his friends" Then ask your child what they think will happen.

TIPS FOR MANAGING ADHD SYMPTOMS AT SCHOOL

Managing ADHD at school can present a range of challenges, but by using some practical methods, you and your child's teacher can boost their educational success.

- **Minimizing Interruptions**

Controlling the impulse to speak when they should be listening can be tricky for kids with ADHD. As a result, they may shout out in class or talk over others. Challenging these outbursts in front of their peers can be particularly embarrassing and impact their self-esteem. Instead, encourage their teacher to develop a secret signal or word that is used to let them know they are interrupting. Interruption-free lessons should be praised or rewarded.

- **Distractibility**

Kids with ADHD are often easily distracted by things happening in their immediate environment. These could be noises they can hear from outside or across the hall, people coming in or going out of the classroom, and even their own thoughts. Once distracted, they miss or battle to retain the information being shared. In addition, children with ADHD have trouble with tasks that require sustained concentration.

There are four essential things needed to limit distractibility.

1. Seating – kids with ADHD should not sit near windows and doors.
2. Movement – incorporate physical activity into lessons.
3. Information – write information in simple terms for the student to refer to.
4. Assignment size – break assignments into manageable tasks.

- **Managing ADHD Impulsivity**

Often kids with ADHD are seen as aggressive or poorly behaved because they struggle with impulse control and act without thinking.

Managing impulsivity requires a combination of the following techniques:

Written behavior plan – ensure the child has access to this so they can refer to it regularly.

Immediate consequences – poor behavior should be addressed immediately, and a clear explanation given regarding their misbehavior.

Immediate praise and recognition – good behavior should be recognized immediately with confirmation of what they did right.

Written daily schedule – allow the child to cross off each task/activity as completed. Knowing what to expect can help kids with ADHD feel more in control and calm.

- **Fidgeting & Hyperactivity**

Sitting still is not something kids with ADHD find easy to do. The symptoms of this condition can cause them to be in a state of perpetual motion. As a result, staying seated can be virtually impossible.

One way to release this energy is to use this movement appropriately. For example, teachers could ask the child to complete a task, such as cleaning the board or taking a note to the office. Playing sports and actively participating in PE is also great for calming hyperactivity. Parents could purchase stress balls or fidget toys for discreet use in the classroom, limit screen time and encourage physical activity.

WHAT PARENTS SHOULD KNOW

- **Challenges in the classroom**

The classroom can be a challenging and daunting place for a child with ADHD. These kids may seem okay outwardly, but unlike their peers, they struggle with the basics required for effective learning, such as not paying attention or being organized. Unfortunately, this can get them labeled as lazy or careless, which is so far from the truth it's ridiculous!

Sadly, many teachers don't completely understand the difficulties kids with ADHD face. This means we as parents must become the link between our kids and their educators so that they understand the challenges our kids face.

- **The ADHD child's rights at school**

Children with ADHD may be eligible for an IEP (Individualized Education Program) tailor-made to suit their academic needs. However, in some cases, they may not qualify for an IEP plan but still require additional support; in this instance 504 plan could be more beneficial. See the above sections on IEPs and 504 plans.

- **Identifying strengths and capitalizing on them**

So often, ADHD is seen as an 'issue' because of the negative symptoms associated with the condition. However, kids with ADHD have particular strengths that others aren't able to tap into as easily. For example, being able to focus intently on tasks they enjoy, also known as 'hyperfocus.' This can be especially beneficial for the school environment. In addition, other strengths such as quick thinking, the ability to multi-task at speed, and creative thinking can be encouraged in the classroom and used to enhance their educational journey.

- **Changing strategies as per need**

Of course, no two children with ADHD are the same. This means that specific teaching strategies may work for one child, but an entirely different approach is required for another. Unfortunately, with ADHD, there is no one size fits all approach! Instead, parents and educators should work together to implement strategies that enhance a child's education based on their bespoke and changing needs.

HOW TEACHERS CAN HELP

- **Classroom teaching strategies for ADHD children**

Two school-based management strategies can be effective when teaching children with ADHD.

Behavioral classroom management

This management strategy is teacher-led and involves the use of a reward system or daily report card. For example, teachers can use a star chart on the board to encourage good behaviors and discourage negative ones. This positive reinforcement can increase student engagement and academic results.

Organization training

This training teaches children organizational skills such as time management, assignment planning, and keeping track of their school materials.

Teachers, counselors, and other educators usually follow the IEP or 504 plan to teach and encourage these positive behaviors.

- **Communication**

Communication is important when teaching kids with ADHD. Sudden changes in routine and insensitive feedback can negatively impact their learning. In addition, kids with ADHD may require a little extra in terms of classroom assistance daily.

Teachers should:

◇ Be sensitive to the impact of ADHD on emotions and feelings – often, those with ADHD have low self-esteem and struggle to regulate their emotions.
◇ Provide regular feedback and focus on the positives, such as good behavior and achievements.
◇ Give fair warning before activities or tasks change, especially regarding changes in routine.

- **Develop a plan that suits the child**

No two children are the same; therefore, a learning plan should meet your child's bespoke needs. Teachers can observe and provide vital information when developing an IEP or implementing learning strategies beneficial to your child.

To gain this information, they can do the following:

They can observe and chat with the student about what distracts them or helps them focus while learning. For example, fidget toys can help with concentration, but background music may be too distracting. They should also discuss the student's needs with the school psychologist or counselor and have regular catch-up sessions with the parents, providing feedback regarding behavior and progress.

A successful learning plan must consider all aspects of your child's life. This includes their classroom environment, home life, and social interactions.

- **Parent education and support**

If there's one thing I can't reiterate enough, it's the power of knowledge. Knowledge of this chronic condition, its effects, and how it impacts our children is the only way to bring the ADHD beast to its knees. Empower yourself with every piece of information you can find because once you understand ADHD, you can empower your children to live successful lives.

CHADD (Children and Adults with Attention Deficit Disorder) is an excellent place to start. This CDC-funded program provides parents with a wealth of information and advice on ADHD. Besides a dedicated ADHD helpline, they also provide fact sheets on ADHD, videos, podcasts, weekly newsletters, and professional training for educators and care providers.

- **Advocating our children**

Below are a few ways to advocate for your child and ensure they get the most from their education journey.

◇ Understand ADHD, its impact on education, and how you can help at home.
◇ Play an active part in your child's 504 Plan or IEP.
◇ Familiarize yourself with your child's IEP, and ask questions if you are unsure.
◇ Raise any concerns about your child's progress, IEP, or 504 plan.
◇ Know your parental rights
◇ Keep records regarding assessments, evaluations, and communication between you and the school.
◇ Have regular meetings with your child's teacher.
◇ Encourage good learning and homework habits, and create a plan to help with tasks and projects.

◇ Maintain a good relationship with the school but be firm in supporting your child.

As the parent of a child with ADHD, I can honestly say a lot of the work is down to us parents. Our efforts play an integral role in providing the best education for our children. In fact, we are the link between our kids and their educators.

THE SELF-LOVING PARENT

"Self-compassion is simply giving the same kindness to ourselves that we would give to others."

— CHRISTOPHER GERMER

The doorbell rang incessantly; someone on the other side must either have an emergency or desperately need my attention. Either way, I was going to let them have a 'piece of Lina Coles' mind! How were they managing to sound so frantic simply by pressing that small button? All this filtered through my thoughts as I stepped over my son's toy truck, navigated the lego maze in the hallway, and launched myself at the door.

Looking back, I see now that the poor postman got more than he bargained for when he rang that doorbell three times in a row! Concerned about leaving a parcel on the porch, he rang a few times to check if I was home, thinking I may have been out in the backyard with the kids. Charlie is nice that way, such a considerate postman, except today he was about to pay for his nice-ness in ways he possibly hadn't considered while standing in the doorway of his good friend Lina!

The apparition that presented to him as I threw the door open should have been enough to have him back down the stairs. Instead, he stood there and absorbed the scene in front of him like a deer caught in the headlights! My unbrushed hair was having one of its frizzy (wild woman) days, no makeup adorned my face, and to say I was dressed would be a stretch.

My clothing (PJs) was stained with orange juice, smears of jam toast, and something that may have been egg but was possibly snot. No, I wasn't sick or struggling from a mental breakdown (yes, I was!). This was me after a bad morning of tearful, screaming ADHD temper tantrums, missed morning shower, and housework that never seemed to end. Poor Charlie got the full blast of my frustration, yelling and screaming. I asked him what the heck he thought he was doing ringing the bell for so long? The poor chap scuttled out the yard without replying!

As I closed the door, I leaned against it and slid down to sit on the floor, too exhausted to face another round of screaming and yelling. I was absolutely done in, and there was no one to blame but myself. As a result of my poor self-care, I had just vented my frustration on a dear friend, and if I'm honest, it was also the cause of the messy tantrums I had been grappling with that day. My patience was at its lowest; I felt totally undermined and angry at my inability to get my son to listen. Worse still, I'm ashamed to say; that I resented my son! When last had I had a minute to myself? I couldn't even answer this question because the truth was, I never made time for myself.

THE IMPORTANCE OF SELF-CARE

Too often, we parents are so busy 'managing' everything that we forget one important element of parenting – self-care. It's worse for parents that have kids with ADHD because we are so busy trying not to upset their routines and maintain the structure they crave that we forget about ourselves. Consider this for one second, if you became ill, who would look after your child? Mental illness, anxiety, and other health issues can result from poor self-care. Consequently, the care we give our kids is affected or limited. It's a sobering thought to think that how we care for ourselves can directly impact the care we provide for our children.

Therefore, it makes sense that mentally and physically exhausted parents will struggle to provide adequate care for their kids with ADHD. Yes, you might cover the basics such as food, basic hygiene etcetera but exhaustion often means our levels of patience, empathy, and kindness go out the window, this can negatively impact our kid's behavior, and I don't have to tell you how chaotic this can make your home! Don't feel bad about this; it's perfectly 'human,' but it also means we need to do something about it to remain the superhero parents we are striving to be!

HOW DOES SELF-CARE BENEFIT PARENTING?

- Self-care restores health, focus, and positivity

Parenting kids with ADHD is very demanding, mentally, physically, and emotionally. Aside from the usual demands kids make on our time, kids with ADHD require additional support. As parents, this can be emotionally overwhelming and directly impact our mental health, especially if we fall into the trap of sacrificing our own needs to meet theirs.

I'm not suggesting we stop putting our kid's needs first; that would be unnatural. But instead, we need to recognize that we as parents also have needs that, when met, allow us to parent our kids effectively and prevent us from becoming emotionally overwrought and resentful.

A healthy lifestyle requires balance. Besides diet and exercise, balance is also required for work and play. Just as you need to work to pay bills, parent your kids and keep your home tidy, you also need to 'work' at having time off!

- It allows parents to manage their kids better and set clear boundaries

Our kids aren't being selfish when they demand our attention constantly. Unfortunately, they are still developmentally immature and don't realize that our energy and focus are not limitless. Quite simply, they believe their parents are like the superheroes they read about, in-exhaustible! And where do they get this idea from? Sadly, they get this from us because we go to great lengths to meet their needs, even at the cost of ourselves.

Setting boundaries that clearly define time for your kids and time for you is not selfish; it's necessary.

- It's a great way to reconnect with your kid on a positive note

The more time you make for yourself, the more positive energy you will have to channel into your parenting techniques and, ultimately, your child. It's about finding a balance between your needs and your child's needs. Once you have achieved this balance, life becomes simpler, happier, and less stressful. Remember, you are entitled to a life too. Just because you are a parent to a child with ADHD doesn't mean you are required to sacrifice yourself on the proverbial altar of ADHD.

PRACTICING SELF-CARE STRATEGIES FOR PARENTS

Practicing self-care shouldn't be another 'item to do' on your endless list of chores and errands. Instead, it should be part of your daily life; learning what it takes to keep you centered will help you feel less like you are about to spin out of control.

Practicing self-care relieves stress, improves social interaction, boosts our productivity, and makes us better parents. Of course, self-care looks different to each of us; while I love to soak in a hot tub after a long day, my hubby prefers to hit the gym. It's about finding what works for you and repeating the process regularly!

- **Take a day off**

A day off from parenting? Who's permission would you need? Only yours, of course! Arrange childcare or ask your partner to step in so you can take the day off and spend quality time with yourself. No chores or errands allowed! Make plans or don't, but whatever you do, spend the time focused on restoring your body and mind.

- **Spend some "me" time**

Perhaps a whole day off isn't possible? It's still possible to set aside a small chunk of time to relax and unwind. It doesn't need to be more than an hour, and you can easily slot this in while the kids are at school or during after school activities! Go for a walk/run, sit in the park with a takeaway coffee or soak in the tub with a good book and herbal tea. The possibilities are endless; remember to turn that parent brain off and take time to enjoy the solitude!

- **Spend time outdoors**

Spending time outdoors is excellent for mental health. Pop into the garden or go for a walk at a local park and spend time absorbing the sun, fresh air, and nature. Grab an ice cream along the way and spend a decadent half hour all to yourself!

- **Get social**

Parenting doesn't leave much time for dinners, phone calls with family and friends, or even a cheeky night out with the guys or girls. This means these activities require planning and structuring (something you're an expert at now!) Scheduling these activities into your diary is a great self-care strategy and gives you something to look forward to!

- **Treat yourself**

Often, we parents forget the basics we need, such as new clothes or shoes, a decent haircut, or even a much-needed coat. In the chaos of ensuring that our kids have everything, we forget we need things too. So the next time you go shopping for yourself and find yourself sifting through t-shirts or other items for the kids, remember to give yourself some space and time to get the shoes you've been eyeing or that summer dress you need. Treating yourself shows your kids you have value too!

- **Exercise**

Not many of us get the time to exercise juggling busy parenting routines, but the benefits of it are too important to ignore. Just 5 minutes of regular aerobic exercise can decrease stress, improve sleep and help reduce anxiety! It also promotes the release of endorphins (feel-good brain chemicals) that enhances your mood and happiness.

- **Spend time reading books**

Books are a great way to escape into another dimension away from the messy chaos of parenting! But aside from this, they also help with mental agility as we age, increase our creativity, improve sleep and hone our empathy skills. Reading is also a great way to reduce mental stress!

The local library or bookstore are great places to start searching for your favorite author. Alternatively, join a book club; it's an excellent way to ensure you stick to your reading schedule and gain a new perspective on things while meeting up with people outside your usual parenting circle. However, if you prefer reading in solitude, you could also set up a kindle or ebook account and start reading online today!

- **Get proper sleep**

It can be challenging to get a good night's sleep, especially for parents who have kids struggling with ADHD sleep disturbances. Sometimes simply 'getting' to sleep is the hardest part of the process! Unfortunately, we know that poor sleep patterns affect ADHD symptoms, but they also impact parents and their parenting skills. No one, not even Superman, can deal well with their child's ADHD symptoms when overtired from lack of sleep! Stick to a bedtime routine each night and if that doesn't work, have a quick cat nap when the kids are at school or resting.

- **Have a word with your partner**

Often the first thing to suffer when parenting kids with ADHD is our communication with our partners. This isn't sciency gubbins I'm sprouting here; I'm speaking from experience. As each of you strives to give the best care to your child, you may find that you're both constantly 'too busy' to sit down and have a basic conversation.

While it's important to spend time discussing your child and their challenges, it's also vital that you make time to chat about yourselves!

You are still entitled to dream about the future and have a loving relationship. Putting yourselves last all the time can put tremendous strain on a relationship, especially when dealing with the stress of ADHD.

Schedule a regular once-a-month date night, even if it's just PJs and a takeaway on the couch. Watch a movie together or take a romantic evening walk. It doesn't matter what you do; it's about spending quality time together. This also enables you to present a united, positive front when faced with the onslaught of ADHD! It's also an excellent time to bring up those days off, compare diaries, and book that 'me time' I was talking about!

- **Meditate**

Meditation quietens the mind, relaxes the body, and relieves stress. Factoring in a few minutes of meditation daily can help control anxiety and promote emotional stability. Sound peaceful? Here's how to slot a smidge of meditation into your otherwise hectic life; all you need is 5-minutes!

Step 1 – set a timer on your phone for 5-minutes.

Step 2 – relax your body, close your eyes and take some slow deep breaths.

Step 3 – continue breathing slowly, clear your mind, and try not to think of anything.

Step 4 – allow thoughts to filter in but then let them go, returning your focus to the present moment of simply being and breathing.

Step 5 – continue this process until the 5-minutes are up, focusing on the sensations you are feeling and letting the stress go.

- **Listen to music**

Music influences how we feel; you only have to listen to Pharell William's song Happy to believe this statement! I bet you started instinctively tapping your foot! This is because listening to music we enjoy reduces stress and anxiety and improves our mood. It's also a great way to relax and unwind while practicing a little self-care. So play your favorite play-list or CD on your way to work or while relaxing in the garden. Or pump up the tunes while cooking dinner; it's bound to get you feeling much more 'in tune' with yourself!

- **Maintain a gratitude journal**

Gratitude journals are a dedicated space (online, physical paper diary) used to express appreciation for the good things in your life. These don't have to be material things and can range from a beautiful sunrise to the help you received from a good friend.

You may even be grateful for your child's progress at school or the fact they did well on a test! It's too easy to become engrossed in the negative things impacting our lives; as a result, we neglect to notice the good stuff. Using a gratitude journal can also help you see things in a positive way, even when things are tough. This builds mental resilience, and when faced with difficulties, we start to see them as opportunities for growth.

Gratitude journals can include:

- 1-3 things you are grateful for daily
- Quotes or positive affirmations
- Questions/journal prompts that promote joy, positivity, and appreciation

- **Engage your senses**

Touch, taste, sound, smell, and sight are the five senses we use to navigate life. They are the essence of what it is to be human. Without them, life would be empty, especially if all five were missing! Being mindful of our senses can help enrich self-care strategies. Try a few of these activities and actively engage your senses; notice how you feel each time.

Sight – visit an art gallery, walk in nature, look at old photos

Smell – use aromatherapy, scented candles, essential oils

Sound – listen to classical music, soothing melodies, rock music?

Taste – eat foods that are spicy, sweet, or savory

Touch – have a massage, hug a loved one, hold hands with your partner

Each of these senses has the power to invoke good memories or feelings as we indulge in these self-care activities. Notice which senses are engaged in activities that make you feel good, then do more of them!

Giving as much time to yourself as you give to your child is not selfish; it's healthy self-care. It provides you with the space to reset your mind and energy levels. Good self-care strategies ensure your emotional, mental, and physical health is in perfect synergy. In summary, good self-care boosts your parenting skills into uber-parenting plans!

13

NO MAN IS AN ISLAND

"Accepting Help Is Its Own Kind Of Strength."

— KIERA CASS

The other day while standing at the checkout, I noticed an elderly gentleman struggling with a heavy grocery basket. As I was about to offer assistance, the basket handle gave away and deposited his precious shopping across the floor. The poor dear looked mortified and hurriedly started collecting the fallen items, jamming them back into the shopping basket. Of course, by this point, I was also chasing errant oranges and runaway shampoo bottles that were rolling around on the floor!

As I returned from the frozen food aisle with his canned peas and safety pins, I could hear him repeatedly saying to everyone helping him, "I'm so sorry, please leave it; I can do this myself."

I did wonder at the time why he was finding it so hard to accept the help he obviously needed. How on earth did he think he could dash in fifty directions at once? At the time, I put it down to being fiercely independent, something that only gets worse with age, I hear!

SUPPORT FOR PARENTS

As parents of kids with ADHD, we are much like this elderly man. Instead of accepting help with the mammoth task of raising our kids, we believe that somehow, we can do this all on our own without the help and support of others. Unfortunately, this leaves us dashing in all directions and accomplishing nothing because exhausted, unwell parents aren't effective against the challenges of ADHD.

Accepting help from others is essential to good parenting and is beneficial for you and your child.

◇ Parents are happier and healthier when supported and can provide better care for their children.
◇ It teaches our kids that asking for help is a positive thing; if you ask for help, they will too.
◇ It allows others to feel needed and included in your life.

TYPES OF SUPPORT

There are three types of support a parent can benefit from, these include:

- **Practical support**

Practical support is to help with the daily management of children. This could range from school transport, homework activities, household chores, shopping, and emergencies. This kind of support is typically provided by those closest to us, for example, grandparents, friends, and neighbors.

Of course, this practical support isn't always available; relatives and friends have their own lives, and grandparents aren't always able. This might mean you need to look at employing someone to help. Parents with kids that have disabilities can also check their government services to see if they are eligible for funding to hire a dedicated support worker.

- **Personal support**

Family and friends can provide you with the space to talk about your feelings and concerns. Good personal support comes from those with your best interests at heart; they realize you need to talk about your frustrations and don't judge or share what you tell them. Other sources of personal support could be parents in similar situations (fellow ADHD combat members!), parents at your child's school, community leaders or religious leaders.

- **Information support**

This is support from professionals, parenting programs, the community, schools, and reliable resources online. The best form of help when parenting kids with ADHD is information support. The more you know about the condition, the more 'in control' you will feel. However, be wary of inaccurate online or media resources as these can confuse things and cause more problems than good. A good rule of thumb is to sense-check anything you are unsure of with your doctor or ADHD-experienced professional.

- **Other support sources**

I like to call these our community-based support sources. Remember I mentioned it takes a village to raise a child? This is where this concept comes to life.

◇ Child care centers/services

These centers allow parents to work and study. This means parents can gain the skills they require for jobs that will help support their children. Of course, child care isn't free and can be quite costly. If you are on a low income, it's a good idea to check if you are eligible for one of the following:

1. State assistance subsidy
2. Tax subsidy
3. Child tax credit
4. Employer subsidy program

◇ Babysitting clubs

Most communities have babysitting services. While this may seem the answer to your prayers, it's a good idea to obtain references to ensure the babysitters are well-known, responsible, and have first aid training. Alternatively, you could set up your own club with other parents of ADHD kids and help each other by sharing babysitting duties.

◇ Libraries

While libraries are an excellent source of information on ADHD, they also provide enjoyable storytelling sessions for parents and kids. Check with your local library when their story sessions are and make it part of your weekly routine. It's also a great way to get them interested in reading and get in some good practice learning to sit quietly!

JOINING A SUPPORT GROUP

We all need a little extra support at times, especially when it comes to parenting children with ADHD. As I mentioned previously, we aren't born with parenting skills, and most of our parenting experience comes from learning on the job. This is okay (sort of) until ADHD makes an unwelcome entrance and all the parenting skills we thought we had, are suddenly rendered useless.

One of the best ways to develop effective parenting skills is to join a parent support group.

What is a parenting support group?

A parenting support group is a group of parents (old hacks) and new who meet up to share their parenting experiences and learn from each other. Here, parents can discuss specific parenting topics, share their concerns and learn healthy parenting skills. These groups aren't only for parents of young children; there are also groups for parents with teens and for parents with children with mental health conditions such as ADHD, anxiety, and depression.

Why join support groups?

As a parent, you probably have had your fair dose of loneliness, especially if you don't have a large group of friends or close family connections. A support group is one of the best ways to combat these feelings while empowering you to be the best parent possible.

- **Self-care**

Even parents with the happiest kids struggle with emotional and physical exhaustion. Usually, this is because we put our own needs last. It's too easy to forget to take care of ourselves while busy raising happy, confident kids. Unfortunately, ignoring our self-care doesn't make it go away; eventually, it catches up with us, and we find ourselves burnt out.

As a result, our energy levels dive through the floorboards along with our empathy levels, leaving us tired, irritated, and lacking the patience required to parent our child successfully. A parenting group promotes self-care, providing a safe space to express your feelings and care for your mental well-being.

- **Help build a support system**

Most parents you meet at parenting support groups have been through exactly what you are going through. They empathize and understand the challenges you face. They also have access to all the information you need. By collaborating with other support group members, you can access the best doctors, caregivers, programs, books, and websites. They will also be able to advise on which of these to avoid!

Support groups are also the perfect place to learn about health conditions commonly associated with ADHD.

- **Help to build skills**

As parents with kids that have ADHD, we learn something new every day! A support group allows you to tap into a wealth of experience-based information you wouldn't find on an internet site or in a medical journal. Fellow parent group members have been in the 'trenches'; they know what it's like to roll up their sleeves and work with ADHD. The parenting tips and techniques they share could quite easily be the answer to your ADHD tantrum woes or challenges you may be having communicating with your teen!

- **Allows opportunity to self-reflect**

Knowing someone else understands what you are going through is like having a large shot in the arm of empathy. Support groups provide a safe, non-judgmental place to reflect on your parenting skills and the challenges you are facing. It's also extremely helpful to receive honest feedback from people who 'get' how difficult ADHD can be. Most importantly, support group members can help you find other options for dealing with behavioral issues and other symptoms associated with ADHD.

TYPES OF SUPPORT GROUPS

Depending on the type of support you need, you may decide to join either a parenting education group or a special needs support group.

- **Parenting education group**

This type of parenting group focuses on providing general guidance and advice to parents and single parents. New parents find these groups particularly useful as they learn from others with more experience. However, these support groups can also be used to improve general parenting skills and improve parent-child relationships.

- **Special needs support group**

These groups provide help and education on raising kids with specific conditions such as ADHD and other mental health conditions. Here parents receive advice on how to parent kids with special needs, access to specialist referrals, and most importantly, support.

When choosing a support group, you must be mindful of what support you need. In other words, attending a support group for parents with teenagers won't be helpful if you have toddlers.

Some support groups meet online, while others meet face-to-face in local libraries or town halls. Depending on your preference, you may decide getting out of the house and meeting up with other parents is more beneficial than logging onto a social media platform. Other parents may feel they can't take the time out and find online meetings fit better into their schedule. Of course, this boils down to what support groups are available in your area; either way, joining a parent support group is a healthy step in the right direction!

HOW TO FIND A SUPPORT GROUP NEAR YOU

There are several ways you can find support groups near you:

◇ Check online for groups based in your area.
◇ Local community centers can recommend groups available to you.
◇ Request a referral from your doctor, pediatrician, or mental health professional.

Best online support groups in America

- **Mad in America**

https://www.madinamerica.com/

Who: Parents with children who have mental health issues

Parents can exchange information and share parenting experiences during a 90-minute meeting. Each meeting can have up to 15 participants and provides a space for parents to discuss diagnosis and treatment methods.

- **Mensgroup.com**

https://mensgroup.com

Who: Male parents looking to improve their parenting skills

Trying to be the provider, protector, and level-headed parent can leave you feeling overwhelmed. This group is for guys looking to learn from the parenting experiences of other men. This online community helps dads become better parents by providing advice and guidance on parenting issues and challenges. Members meet online or chat via text.

- **HOPE** (Helping Other Parents Everywhere)

http://www.hope4parents.ca/

Who: Parents everywhere, including guardians and relatives.

HOPE is an online parent support group that supports those parenting troubled teens and young adults. Carers can share experiences and gain access to specialized help and advice.

Parenting is a skill that is acquired over time; at each developmental stage of your child's life, these skills will need to be adjusted to suit their needs. Asking for help is not shameful nor an indication of your inadequacies as a parent. Instead, it shows strength of character to stand up and say things like "I need help," "can you please advise," and "I don't know." By being willing to learn, recognizing our needs, and accepting help, we can utilize effective parenting strategies and raise successful, positive kids!

LEAVE A 1-CLICK REVIEW!

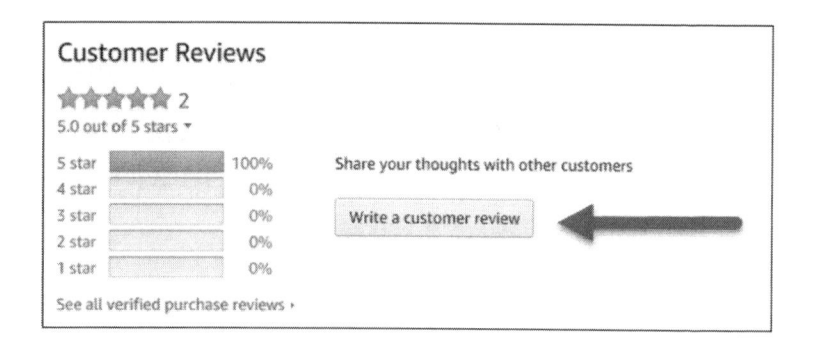

I would be incredibly thankful if you could take just 60 seconds to write a brief review on Amazon, even if it's just a few sentences!

Scan the QR Code below!

CONCLUSION

"There's no such thing as a perfect parent. Just be a real one."

— SUE ATKINS

Sat across the room from my son, I'm watching him straighten his tie and smooth down his hair in the mirror. Of course, everything has to be just perfect, because today is graduation day!

This year, the final year of high school has been challenging, filled with the stress of exams and the frustrations of studying. I'm honestly not sure how we made it! But made it, we did, and today we have arrived at the finish line.

As I watch him getting ready to celebrate his academic success, he flashes me a cheeky grin, eagerly anticipating the next chapter of his life; he's impatient to get to his graduation ceremony. Like most kids his age, my son has big dreams of going to university to study Computer Science, getting his driver's license and back-packing with his friends through Europe.

Of course, this leaves me feeling panicked and anxious about how he will manage and imagining all the terrible things that could possibly happen to him. I suppose I'm just like any other mother out there getting ready to send her child off into the big unknown, and I guess he's like any other son getting ready to spread his wings. Except we're not like those other moms and sons, we have a third member to consider, ADHD.

Just because he's grown up doesn't mean the spectre of ADHD has left us. On the contrary, its cruel fingers will always tamper with the intricacies of my son's mental ability. And while its symptoms are better managed and 'under control', the fact is, it's a condition that will co-exist alongside my son's gorgeous sunny smile and nature for the rest of his life. I hope, though, that you can see from the information I have shared that ADHD isn't the 'life sentence' it's made out to be. Instead, with effective parenting strategies in place, a child with ADHD can develop and mature into a successful adult ready to take on the world, even if you don't feel ready for it!

Sometimes parenting kids with ADHD is so overwhelming that you may feel like giving up. But, as I watch my son today, I'm glad I didn't give up on him. The sense of achievement I feel as I see him chatting confidently with his friends before the ceremony fills me with as much pride as the fantastic grades he's managed to achieve. In addition, his resilience and ability to bounce back from disappointment often leave me dumbfounded. How has this child turned out so well with a parent like me?

I can't pretend that I was/ am the perfect parent. There were meltdowns (many of them mine), temper tantrums (again also mine) and, ashamedly, plenty of moments where I felt ready to walk out and never return. As I mentally run through the list of possible ADHD issues, I think we have ticked most of them off our list over the years. However, we've managed to come out the other side. Most assuredly, this hasn't been easy; it's taken some long hard looks in the mirror, having a positive attitude (death grip on sanity) and realizing there's a lot of help and support for ADHD parents.

Being the best possible parent to your child begins with three simple words. "I need help". When you recognize that you need support, the ADHD puzzle starts to fall into place.

Thankfully our children are living, breathing, vibrant souls. But this also means they can't be squashed into neat little ADHD boxes because each child is unique and wonderfully made. Not every parenting strategy will work for your child; it's about finding the techniques that work for them and then using these to enhance and capitalize on their strengths and abilities.

While you are strategizing and boosting their self-esteem, teaching them how to manage impulses, regulate emotions and, most importantly, be mindful of their manners, remember to forge a solid, healthy, loving relationship with your child. Finally, don't get so lost in the parenting side of things that you forget to enjoy being the parent of an amazing human being!

I hear the music start to play; my son's class is waiting to make their way across the stage to collect their high school diploma. The time has come! I watch as he stands calmly, waiting for his name to be called. I know the patience and control this simple act requires. The tears roll down my face unashamedly as I watch him walk proudly across the stage to accept his ceremonial scroll. For me, this is symbolic of the success he has made of his life while struggling with the challenges of ADHD.

He turns and grins straight at me, "thanks, mom", he mouths silently as he takes his place center stage. It's victories like this that make me realize how wonderful the role of a parent can be. Yes, it's tough, and there will be days when you've lost your temper, shouted at a school official or two (don't ask) and possibly overstepped the mark. But if it's all in the name of advocating for our kids, then it's definitely worth the effort!

Parenting a child with ADHD doesn't have to be a lonely journey; there is help out there; you just need to be willing to accept it! Remember to look after yourself; self-care is vital for effective parenting. Join a support group or forum and start sharing and learning from the experiences of others. It's also an excellent opportunity to share your success stories; who doesn't like to brag about their child a little? Understanding ADHD can help you become a better parent armed with techniques that work.

As a parent or carer of a child with ADHD, you have taken the first step towards becoming a better parent or guardian. By taking the time to understand this chronic condition, you have taken up arms against its crippling symptoms and sounded the official war cry. Let the battle commence!

JUST FOR YOU!

A FREE GIFT TO OUR READERS

Tantrum Soothers

Simply scan the QR code below
to request access to this FREE resource!

RESOURCES PAGE

Data and Statistics About ADHD | CDC. (2020, November 16). Centers for Disease Control and Prevention. https://www.cdc.gov/ncbddd/adhd/data.html

Why is ADHD more common in boys? | ADHD - Sharecare. (n.d.). Sharecare. Retrieved June 21, 2022, from http://www.sharecare.com/health/add-adhd/adhd-more-common-in-boys

Diagnosis of ADHD in Adults - CHADD. (n.d.). CHADD. Retrieved June 21, 2022, from https://chadd.org/for-adults/diagnosis-of-adhd-in-adults

What NOT to Say to the Parent of a Child with ADHD. (2021, September 28). Attitude; ADDitude Editors. https://www.additudemag.com/slideshows/common-myths-about-adhd

Mum. (2017, August 9). *Does poverty cause ADHD or does ADHD cause poverty? My own thoughts.* Website. https://www.families-focussed.co.uk/single-post/2017/08/09/Does-poverty-cause-ADHD-or-does-ADHD-cause-poverty-My-own-thoughts

Rate and predictors of divorce among parents of youth with ADHD - PMC. (n.d.). PubMed Central (PMC). Retrieved June 21, 2022, from https://www.ncbi.nlm.nih.gov/pmc/articles/PMC2631569

Parenting experiences of living with a child with attention deficit hyperactivity disorder: a systematic review of qualitative evidence - PubMed.

(n.d.). PubMed. Retrieved June 21, 2022, from https://pubmed.ncbi.nlm.nih.gov/26657468

A review of the economic burden of ADHD - PMC. (n.d.). PubMed Central (PMC). Retrieved June 21, 2022, from https://www.ncbi.nlm.nih.gov/pmc/articles/PMC1180839

Focused Mind ADHD Counseling - Therapist in Columbus Ohio - 43220. (n.d.). William Roberts. Retrieved June 21, 2022, from https://focusedmindadhdcounseling.com

Frances E. KuoPhD, & Andrea Faber TaylorPhD. (2011, October 11). *A Potential Natural Treatment for Attention-Deficit/Hyperactivity Disorder: Evidence From a National Study.* AJPH. https://ajph.aphapublications.org/doi/full/10.2105/AJPH.94.9.1580

Hoogman,PHD, D. M., Bralten,PHD, J., Hibar,PHD, D., & Mennes, PHD, M. (n.d.). *Subcortical brain volume differences in participants with attention deficit hyperactivity disorder in children and adults: a crosssectional mega-analysis.* The Lancet Psychiatry. Retrieved June 21, 2022, from https://secure.jbs.elsevierhealth.com/action/getSharedSiteSession?rc=1&redirect=https%3A%2F%2Fwww.thelancet.com%2Fjournals%2Flanpsy%2Farticle%2FPIIS2215-0366%2817%2930049-4%2Ffulltext

Data and Statistics About ADHD | CDC. (2020, November 16). Centers for Disease Control and Prevention.https://www.cdc.gov/ncbddd/adhd/data.html

High levels of dopamine may lead to increased risk-taking. (2015, July 7). Science Daily. https://www.sciencedaily.com/releases/2015/07/150707213245.htm

Duggal, N. (2021, August 31). *ADHD and Dopamine: What's the Connection?* Healthline; Healthline Media. https://www.healthline.com/health/adhd/adhd-dopamine#connection

Thomas, S. (2019, December 17). *Effort Self-Talk Benefits the Mathematics Performance of Children With Negative Competence Beliefs.* SRCD. https://srcd.onlinelibrary.wiley.com/doi/10.1111/cdev.13347

Fox, J. R., & Martin, H. E. (2017). *Academic Advising and the First College Year.* The National Resource Center for The First-Year Experience.
https://www.perts.net/static/documents/yeager_2014.pdf

Boring but Important: A Self-Transcendent Purpose for Learning Fosters Academic Self-Regulation - PMC. (n.d.). PubMed Central (PMC). Retrieved June 21, 2022, from https://www.ncbi.nlm.nih.gov/pmc/articles/PMC4643833

Attention-Deficit / Hyperactivity Disorder (ADHD) in Children | Johns Hopkins Medicine. (n.d.). Johns Hopkins Medicine, Based in Baltimore, Maryland. Retrieved June 21, 2022, from https://www.hopkinsmedicine.org/health/conditions-and-diseases/adhdadd

Causes of ADHD: What We Know Today - HealthyChildren.org. (n.d.). HealthyChildren.Org. Retrieved June 21, 2022, from https://www.healthychildren.org/English/health-issues/conditions/adhd/Pages/Causes-of-ADHD.aspx

Data and Statistics About ADHD | CDC. (2020, November 16). Centers for Disease Control and Prevention. https://www.cdc.gov/ncbddd/adhd/data.html

Parental ADHD Symptomology and Ineffective Parenting: The Connecting Link of Home Chaos - PMC. (n.d.). PubMed Central (PMC). Retrieved June 21, 2022, from https://www.ncbi.nlm.nih.gov/pmc/articles/PMC2864040/

Symptoms and Diagnosis of ADHD | CDC. (2020, September 21). Centers for Disease Control and Prevention. https://www.cdc.gov/ncbddd/adhd/diagnosis.html

website. (1 C.E.). *Attention deficit hyperactivity disorder (ADHD) - Diagnosis - NHS.* Nhs.Uk. https://www.nhs.uk/conditions/attention-deficit-hyperactivity-disorder-adhd/diagnosis/

When Parent and Child Both Have ADHD - Child Mind Institute. (n.d.). Child Mind Institute. Retrieved June 21, 2022, from https://childmind.org/article/help-for-parents-with-adhd/

ADHD | Behavior Problems in Children | Learning Issues | Child Anxiety | Understood. (n.d.). Understood - For Learning and Thinking Differences. Retrieved June 21, 2022, from https://www.understood.org/en/articles/does-adhd-raise-risk-mental-health-issues

ADHD and Behavior Problems - Child Mind Institute. (n.d.). Child Mind Institute. Retrieved June 21, 2022, from https://childmind.org/article/adhd-behavior-problems/

Lovering, N. (2022, April 21). *ADHD Stigma: Breaking the Silence I Psych Central.* Psych Central; Psych Central. https://psychcentral.com/adhd/breaking-the-silence-of-adhd-stigma#effects-of-stigma

Parenting experiences of living with a child with attention deficit hyperactivity disorder: a systematic review of qualitative evidence - PubMed.

(n.d.). PubMed. Retrieved June 21, 2022, from https://pubmed.ncbi.nlm.nih.gov/26657468/

PhD, J. C. B. I., & PsyD, N. V. B. (2022, March 17). *ADHD—or Something Else?* Psychiatric Times; Psychiatric Times. https://www.psychiatrictimes.com/view/adhd-or-something-else-

Porter, E. (2021, August 9). *Misdiagnosis: Conditions That Mimic ADHD.* Healthline; Healthline Media. https://www.healthline.com/health/adhd/adhd-misdiagnosis

Poulton, A. (2021, June 22). *Myths and stigma about ADHD contribute to poorer mental health for those affected.* The Conversation; https://facebook.com/ConversationEDU. https://theconversation.com/myths-and-stigma-about-adhd-contribute-to-poorer-mental-health-for-those-affected-161591

Dr Sam Goldstein. (n.d.). Dr. Sam Goldstein. Retrieved June 21, 2022, from https://samgoldstein.com/resources/articles/general/a-history-of-executive-functioning-as-a-theoretical-and-clinical-construct.aspx

9 FREE Executive Functioning Activities - The Pathway 2 Success. (2020, July 6). The Pathway 2 Success; https://www.facebook.com/Pathway2Success1/. https://www.thepathway2success.com/9-free-executive-functioning-activities/

ADHD & Stress: Information for Parents - CHADD. (n.d.). CHADD. Retrieved June 21, 2022, from https://chadd.org/adhd-and-covid-19-toolkit/adhd-stress-information-for-parents/

ADHD & the Brain. (n.d.). AACAP Home. Retrieved June 21, 2022, from https://www.aacap.org/AACAP/Families_and_Youth/Facts_for_Families/FFF-Guide/ADHD_and_the_Brain-121.aspx

Ariane. (2022, January 3). *What Is Executive Dysfunction in ADHD?* Verywell Mind; Verywell Mind. https://www.verywellmind.com/what-is-executive-dysfunction-in-adhd-5213034

Ellis, R. R. (9 C.E.). *The 15 Best Exercises to Manage ADHD Symptoms.* WebMD; WebMD. https://www.webmd.com/add-adhd/exercise-manage-adhd-symptoms

Executive Functioning | ADHD Australia. (n.d.). Home Page | ADHD Australia. Retrieved June 21, 2022, from https://www.adhdaustralia.org.au/about-adhd/the-role-of-executive-functioning-in-adhd/

Hacking Your Executive Function: What the Heck is Inhibition? – Aut of Spoons. (2018, October 15). Aut of Spoons; https://www.facebook.com/WordPresscom. https://autofspoons.com/2018/10/15/hacking-your-executive-function-what-the-heck-is-inhibition/#:~:text=It%20is%20resisting%20temptations%20and%20ignoring%20distractions.%20Inhibition,the%20course%20of%20action%20that%20you%20do%20want.

How to reduce stress and improve your executive functioning. -. (2020a, April 22). Connections in Mind; https://www.facebook.com/connectionsinmind/. https://connectionsinmind.com/stress_executivefunctions/

How to reduce stress and improve your executive functioning. -. (2020b, April 22). Connections in Mind; https://www.facebook.com/connectionsinmind/. https://connectionsinmind.com/stress_executivefunctions/

http://ljournal.ru/wp-content/uploads/2016/08/d-2016-154.pdf. (2016). ljournal. http://dx.doi.org/10.18411/d-2016-154

PhD, E. S. (2018, February 12). *How Stress Works With and Against Your Memory*. Verywell Mind; Verywell Mind. https://www.verywellmind.com/stress-and-your-memory-4158323

Practicing Executive Functioning Skills with Play Activities - The Pathway 2 Success. (2018, September 16). The Pathway 2 Success; https://www.facebook.com/Pathway2Success1/. https://www.thepathway2success.com/practicing-executive-functioning-skills-with-play-activities/

Shifting- Cognitive Ability. (2017, January 17). Shifting- Cognitive Ability.https://www.cognifit.com/science/cognitive-skills/shifting

The ADHD Brain | Understood. (n.d.). Understood - For Learning and Thinking Differences. Retrieved June 21, 2022, from https://www.understood.org/en/articles/adhd-and-the-brain

The Effects of Acute Stress on Core Executive Functions: A Meta-Analysis and Comparison with Cortisol - PMC. (n.d.). PubMed Central (PMC). Retrieved June 21, 2022, from https://www.ncbi.nlm.nih.gov/pmc/articles/PMC5003767/

Using Task Cards to Teach Executive Functioning - The Pathway 2 Success. (2017, July 25). The Pathway 2 Success; https://www.facebook.com/Pathway2Success1/. https://www.thepathway2success.com/using-task-cards-to-teach-executive-functioning/

What are some ways to reduce stress with ADHD? - ADHD Awareness Month - October 2022. (2020, October 2). ADHD Awareness Month -

October 2022. https://www.adhdawarenessmonth.org/reduce-stress-with-adhd/

what is cognative flexibility executive function - Search. (n.d.). Bing. Retrieved June 21, 2022, from https://www.bing.com/search?q=what+is+cognative+flexibility+executive+function&qs=n&form=QBRE&sp=-1&pq=what+is+cognative+flexibility+executive+func&sc=1-44&sk=&cvid=D2AEC902F38F4474BD29EA735C78E7D8

What is Executive Function? How Executive Functioning Skills Affect Early Development. (n.d.). Center on the Developing Child at Harvard University. Retrieved June 21, 2022, from https://developingchild.harvard.edu/resources/what-is-executive-function-and-how-does-it-relate-to-child-development/

Working Memory - Cognitive Skill. (2016, June 8). Working Memory - Cognitive Skill. https://www.cognifit.com/science/cognitive-skills/working-memory

ADHD, Self-Harm, and Suicide - CHADD. (n.d.). CHADD. Retrieved June 21, 2022, from https://chadd.org/attention-article/adhd-self-harm-and-suicide/

Developing Social Skills - Thriving with ADHD. (n.d.). Thriving with ADHD; https://www.facebook.com/thrivingwithadhd/. Retrieved June 21, 2022, from https://thrivingwithadhd.com.au/developing-social-skills/

Diagnosing ADHD in Adolescence - CHADD. (n.d.). CHADD. Retrieved June 21, 2022, from https://chadd.org/for-parents/diagnosing-adhd-in-adolescence/

Gender differences in attention-deficit/hyperactivity disorder - PubMed. (n.d.). PubMed. Retrieved June 21, 2022, from https://pubmed.ncbi.nlm.nih.gov/20385342/

Helping Kids and Teens Who Struggle with Executive Functioning Skills - The Pathway 2 Success. (2021, April 20). The Pathway 2 Success; https://www.facebook.com/Pathway2Success1/. https://www.thepathway2success.com/helping-kids-and-teens-who-struggle-with-executive-functioning-skills/

(2020, October 18). *Executive Functioning Activities: 50 Skill Builders for Kids of All Ages!* The Homeschool Resource Room. https://thehomeschoolresourceroom.com/2020/10/17/executive-functioning-activities/

How Girls With ADHD Are Different | Child Mind Institute. (n.d.). Child Mind Institute. Retrieved June 21, 2022, from https://childmind.org/article/how-girls-with-adhd-are-different/

Janice. (2020, February 24). *Helping a child with ADHD develop social skills - Mayo Clinic Health System.* Mayo Clinic Health System; Mayo Clinic Health System. https://www.mayoclinichealthsystem.org/hometown-health/speaking-of-health/helping-a-child-with-adhd-develop-social-skills

Managing ADHD: teenagers 12-18 years | Raising Children Network. (2021, July 5). Raising Children Network. https://raisingchildren.net.au/teens/development/adhd/managing-adhd-12-18-years

Merrill, S. (2021, March 12). *8 Ways to Bolster Executive Function in Teens and Tweens | Edutopia.* Edutopia; George Lucas Educational Foundation. https://www.edutopia.org/article/8-ways-bolster-executive-function-teens-and-tweens

Pagán, C. N. (4 C.E.). *The Link Between Adult ADHD and Risky Behavior*. WebMD; WebMD. https://www.webmd.com/add-adhd/guide/adhd-dangerous-risky-behavior

Parenting Teens with ADHD - CHADD. (n.d.). CHADD. Retrieved June 21, 2022, from https://chadd.org/for-parents/parenting-teens-with-adhd/

Pietrangelo, A. (2021, May 1). *ADHD Symptoms in Teens, Diagnosis, Treatment, and Coping*. Healthline; Healthline Media. https://www.healthline.com/health/adhd/adhd-symptoms-in-teens

ADHD Nutrition: A Healthy Diet for Kids | Jill Castle MS, RDN. (2021, July 9). The Nourished Child; https://www.facebook.com/thenourishedchild/. https://thenourishedchild.com/healthy-adhd-diet-kids/

Attention-deficit/hyperactivity disorder (ADHD) in children - Diagnosis and treatment - Mayo Clinic. (2019, June 25). Mayo Clinic - Mayo Clinic. https://www.mayoclinic.org/diseases-conditions/adhd/diagnosis-treatment/drc-20350895

Elimination Diets for ADHD: Do They Work? | Everyday Health. (n.d.). EverydayHealth.Com. Retrieved June 21, 2022, from https://www.everydayhealth.com/adhd/whats-the-deal-with-elimination-diets-for-adhd/

Gotter, A. (2022, March 16). *Behavioral Therapy: Definition, Types & Effectiveness*. Healthline; Healthline Media. https://www.healthline.com/health/behavioral-therapy

Jain, Kriti. (n.d.). *Diet to control Attention Deficit Hyperactivity*

Disorder. Medindia; Medindia. Retrieved June 21, 2022, from https://www.medindia.net/patients/lifestyleandwellness/diet-to-control-attention-deficit-hyperactivity-disorder.htm

Melinda. (2018, November 2). *Treatment for Children with ADHD - HelpGuide.org*. HelpGuide.Org. https://www.helpguide.org/articles/add-adhd/treatment-for-childhood-attention-deficit-disorder-adhd.htm

Side Effects of ADHD Medication | Child Mind Institute. (n.d.). Child Mind Institute. Retrieved June 21, 2022, from https://childmind.org/article/side-effects-of-adhd-medication/

website. (1 C.E.). *Attention deficit hyperactivity disorder (ADHD) - Treatment - NHS*. Nhs.Uk. https://www.nhs.uk/conditions/attention-deficit-hyperactivity-disorder-adhd/treatment/

12 Ways To Learn To Control Your Emotional Impulses - Self Development Secrets. (n.d.). Self Development Secrets; https://www.facebook.com/selfdevelopmentsecrets. Retrieved June 21, 2022, from https://www.selfdevelopmentsecrets.com/control-emotional-impulses/#:~:text=Continuous%20muscle%20relaxation%20can%20help%20you%20calm%20down,15%20minutes%20in%20a%20quiet%20and%20comfortable%20space.

Associations between abuse/neglect and ADHD from childhood to young adulthood: A prospective nationally-representative twin study - PMC. (n.d.). PubMed Central (PMC). Retrieved June 21, 2022, from https://www.ncbi.nlm.nih.gov/pmc/articles/PMC6013278/

Associations between ADHD and emotional problems from childhood to young adulthood: a longitudinal genetically sensitive study - PubMed.

(n.d.). PubMed. Retrieved June 21, 2022, from https://pubmed.ncbi.nlm.nih.gov/32112575/

Crawford, J. (2018, April 25). *Parenting tips for ADHD: 21 ways to help*. Medical and Health Information; Medical News Today. https://www.medicalnewstoday.com/articles/321621#twenty-one-parenting-tips

Expert, S. S., PsyD, GoodTherapy. org Topic. (2018, March 27). *GoodTherapy | 7 Ways to Help a Child Heal from Trauma*. GoodTherapy.Org Therapy Blog; GoodTherapy.org. https://www.goodtherapy.org/blog/7-ways-to-help-child-heal-from-trauma-0327185

Kandola, A. (2020, November 27). *Emotional distress: What are the causes and symptoms?* Medical and Health Information; Medical News Today. https://www.medicalnewstoday.com/articles/emotional-distress#causes

Key, A. P. (4 C.E.). *ADHD in Children: Managing Moods and Emotions*. WebMD; WebMD. https://www.webmd.com/add-adhd/adhd-children-mood-swings

Low, K. (2008, August 8). *Children With ADHD and Anger*. Verywell Mind; Verywell Mind. https://www.verywellmind.com/understanding-adhd-children-and-anger-20540

Melinda. (2018, November 2). *Helping Children Cope with Traumatic Events - HelpGuide.org*. HelpGuide.Org. https://www.helpguide.org/articles/ptsd-trauma/helping-children-cope-with-traumatic-stress.htm

Miller, G. (2021, July 22). *ADHD Parenting: 12 Tips to Tackle Common Challenges | Psych Central*. Psych Central; Psych Central. https://psychcentral.com/childhood-adhd/parenting-kids-with-adhd-tips-to-tackle-common-challenges

Nelson, A. (7 C.E.). *Is It ADHD or Childhood Traumatic Stress? How to Tell?* WebMD; WebMD. https://www.webmd.com/add-adhd/childhood-adhd/adhd-traumatic-childhood-stress

Parent Training in Behavior Management for ADHD | CDC. (2020, September 23). Centers for Disease Control and Prevention. https://www.cdc.gov/ncbddd/adhd/behavior-therapy.html

Ruiz, R. (2014, July 7). *How Childhood Trauma Could Be Mistaken for ADHD - The Atlantic.* The Atlantic; https://www.facebook.com/TheAtlantic/. https://www.theatlantic.com/health/archive/2014/07/how-childhood-trauma-could-be-mistaken-for-adhd/373328/

Scriver, A. (2020, April 28). *I Never Suspected ADHD Could Be Linked to My Childhood Trauma.* Healthline; Healthline Media. https://www.healthline.com/health/adhd/adhd-linked-to-trauma

Social and emotional difficulties in children with ADHD and the impact on school attendance and healthcare utilization | Child and Adolescent Psychiatry and Mental Health | Full Text. (n.d.). BioMed Central. Retrieved June 21, 2022, from https://capmh.biomedcentral.com/articles/10.1186/1753-2000-6-33

The Lighthouse Counseling. (2020, March 11). *10 Strategies For Coping With Childhood Emotional Neglect.* TLHCOUNSELLING SG; TLHCOUNSELLING SG. https://www.tlhcounselling.com/post/10-strategies-for-coping-with-childhood-emotional-neglect

11 tips on building self-esteem in children. (2020, May 1). Today's

Parent. https://www.todaysparent.com/family/parenting/how-to-build-your-childs-self-esteem/

Contributor, N. M., Lead. (2022, January 21). *4 Causes of Low Self-Esteem in Children | Everyday Power (2020)*. Everyday Power; https://www.facebook.com/EverydayPowerOfficial/. https://everydaypower.com/4-causes-low-self-esteem/

Joleena. (2017, November 10). *How To Help Your Kids Cope With A Narcissistic Parent — Joleena Louis Law*. Joleena Louis Law; Joleena Louis Law. https://www.joleenalouislaw.com/blog/narcissistic-parent

Lee, K. (2016, February 27). *9 Ways to Build More Self-Esteem in Your Child*. Verywell Family; Verywell Family. https://www.verywellfamily.com/ways-to-build-strong-self-esteem-in-your-child-3953464

Prianka. (2017, November 20). *Low Self Esteem In Children Causes: 8 Mistakes Parents Make*. TheAsianparent - Your Guide to Pregnancy, Baby & Raising Kids; theAsianparent. https://sg.theasianparent.com/low-self-esteem-in-children-causes

Self-esteem and teenagers - ReachOut Parents. (n.d.). Home - ReachOut Parents. Retrieved June 21, 2022, from https://parents.au.reachout.com/common-concerns/everyday-issues/self-esteem-and-teenagers

symptoms of narcissism - Search. (n.d.). Bing. Retrieved June 21, 2022, from https://www.bing.com/search?q=symptoms+of+narcissism&FORM=AWRE

5 tips for helping children with ADHD deal with Aggression. (n.d.). HOPE Therapy & Wellness Center | Mental Health Counseling in

Springfield, VA. Retrieved June 21, 2022, from https://www.hopetherapyandwellness.com/blog/115541-5-tips-for-helping-children-with-adhd-deal-with-aggression

ADHD and Temper Tantrums - Health Guide Info. (2010, November 30). Health Guide Info. https://www.healthguideinfo.com/adhd-add-treatment/p97658/#:~:text=ADHD%20and%20Temper%20-Tantrums%201%20Off%20the%20Charts.,Alternatives.%20Families%20who%20are%20managing%20children%20with%20ADHD

ADHD in Children: Understanding, Discipline and Better Parenting. (6 C.E.). OnHealth; OnHealth.https://www.onhealth.com/content/1/parenting_child_adhd

ADHD Symptoms & Behavioral Problems in Children | Drake Institute. (n.d.). ADD, ADHD & Autism Treatment Centers in OC & LA | Drake Institute. Retrieved June 21, 2022, from https://www.drakeinstitute.com/adhd-symptoms-and-behaviors

Amy. (2013, October 4). *Common Child Behavior Problems and Their Solutions.* Verywell Family; Verywell Family. https://www.verywellfamily.com/common-child-behavior-problems-and-their-solutions-1094944

Babich, A. P. (2022, June 14). *The Connection Between ADHD and Sleep Deprivation | Mattress Advisor.* Mattress Advisor | Trusted Reviews, Buying Guides, Sleep Education; Mattress Advisor.https://www.mattressadvisor.com/adhd-and-sleep-deprivation/

Centre. (2021, April 23). *Online ADHD Assessment & Treatments - The ADHD Centre.* The ADHD Centre. https://www.adhdcentre.co.uk

Delfino, D. (2021, July 7). *ADHD and Trouble Sleeping: Is There a Link?* Psych Central; Psych Central. https://psychcentral.com/adhd/adhd-and-sleep-disturbances#common-sleep-disorders

Impulsive Behavior and ADHD - PeoplePsych. (2022, May 12). PeoplePsych; https://www.facebook.com/peoplepsych/. https://peoplepsych.com/impulsive-behavior-and-adhd/

Impulsivity in children | Understood. (n.d.). Understood - For Learning and Thinking Differences. Retrieved June 21, 2022, from https://www.understood.org/en/articles/understanding-impulsivity

Lee, K. (2011, September 20). *7 Effective Ways to Handle Defiant Children.* Verywell Family; Verywell Family. https://www.verywellfamily.com/how-to-handle-defiant-children-620106

Lies & lying: what to do when children lie | Raising Children Network. (2022, February 28). Raising Children Network. https://raisingchildren.net.au/preschoolers/behaviour/common-concerns/lies

Magical Thinking Concept & Examples | What is Magical Thinking? | Study.com. (n.d.). Study.Com. Retrieved June 21, 2022, from https://study.com/learn/lesson/magical-thinking-concept-examples.html

Mercedes. (2019, September 11). *Controlling Screen Time for Children with ADHD.* Psych Central; Psych Central. https://psychcentral.com/lib/controlling-screen-time-for-children-with-adhd#1

Merriam Sarcia Saunders, LMFT. (n.d.). ADDitude. Retrieved June 21, 2022, from https://www.additudemag.com/author/merriam-sarcia-saunders-lmft/

Other Concerns and Conditions with ADHD | CDC. (2020, September 4). Centers for Disease Control and Prevention. https://www.cdc.gov/ncbddd/adhd/conditions.html#BehaviorProblems

Why Kids Lie and What Parents Can Do to Stop It | Child Mind Institute. (n.d.). Child Mind Institute. Retrieved June 21, 2022, from https://childmind.org/article/why-kids-lie/

8 loving ways to show your kid you're the boss. (2021, April 18). Today's Parent. https://www.todaysparent.com/family/discipline/loving-ways-to-show-kid-boss/

10 Effective Ways to be a Positive Role Model for Your Kids. (2019, January 4). FirstCry Parenting; https://www.facebook.com/FirstCryIndia/. https://parenting.firstcry.com/articles/parents-as-a-role-model-shape-your-childs-life-in-a-positive-way/

10 Ways to Be a Role Model to Your Children - All Pro Dad. (2011, September 14). All Pro Dad; https://www.facebook.com/AllProDad. https://www.allprodad.com/10-ways-to-be-a-role-model-to-your-children/

Amy. (2013, January 21). *Role Model the Behavior You Want to See From Your Kids.* Verywell Family; Verywell Family. https://www.verywellfamily.com/role-model-the-behavior-you-want-to-see-from-your-kids-1094785

McCready, A. (2019, March 1). *How to Get Kids to (REALLY) Listen: 7 Steps for Success - Positive Parenting Solutions.* Positive Parenting Solutions; Positive Parenting Solutions. https://www.positiveparentingsolutions.com/parenting/get-kids-to-listen

Parents: role models & influences on teens | Raising Children Network.

(2021, November 5). Raising Children Network. https://raisingchildren.net.au/pre-teens/behaviour/encouraging-good-behaviour/being-a-role-model

Parker, W. (2012, August 10). *Correcting Behavior in a Child Who Won't Listen*. Verywell Family; Verywell Family. https://www.verywellfamily.com/child-discipline-101-kids-wont-listen-1270213

Steber, C. (n.d.). *The Importance of Parents as Role Models*. Thrive; Thrive. Retrieved June 21, 2022, from https://thriveglobal.com/stories/the-importance-of-parents-as-role-models/

The Importance of Teaching Manners to Kids - Child Development Institute. (2011, August 17). Child Development Institute; https://www.facebook.com/ParentingTodayCDI. https://childdevelopmentinfo.com/parenting/the-importance-of-teaching-manners-to-kids/#gs.u1rka2

30 Worst Parenting Mistakes Everyone Makes - Saranga Comprehensive Psychiatry | Holistic Adult Psychiatry in Raleigh and Cary NC. (2018, September 27). Saranga Comprehensive Psychiatry | Holistic Adult Psychiatry in Raleigh and Cary NC. https://www.sarangapsychiatry.com/blog/30-worst-parenting-mistakes-everyone-makes/

Anger & anger management ideas for parents | Raising Children Network. (2020, June 22). Raising Children Network. https://raisingchildren.net.au/guides/first-1000-days/looking-after-yourself/anger-management-for-parents#simple-anger-management-ideas-nav-title

Anger Management: Strategies for Parents and Grandparents. (n.d.). Stanford Children's Health - Lucile Packard Children's Hospital Stanford. Retrieved June 21, 2022, from https://www.stanfordchildrens.org/en/topic/default?id=anger-management-strategies-for-parents-and-grandparents-160-45

FastBraiin. (n.d.). *ADHD and Empathy: Identifying and Resolving the Disconnect– FastBraiin.* FastBraiin. Retrieved June 21, 2022, from https://www.fastbraiin.com/blogs/blog/adhd-and-empathy

Hutchinson, T. (2020, May 25). *7 biggest parenting mistakes that destroy kids' mental strength.* CNBC; CNBC. https://www.cnbc.com/2020/05/25/biggest-parenting-mistake-destroys-kids-mental-strength-says-therapist.html

Taylor, J. (2011, April 22). *Anger Management for Parents - Tips on How to Be a Calm Parent.* Good Housekeeping; Good Housekeeping. https://www.goodhousekeeping.com/life/parenting/tips/a13314/anger-management-parents/

Vincent. (2004, December 19). *11 Common Parenting Mistakes to Avoid.* Verywell Family; Verywell Family. https://www.verywellfamily.com/com mon-parenting-mistakes-2633998

ADHD and School (for Parents) - Nemours KidsHealth. (n.d.). Nemours KidsHealth - the Web's Most Visited Site about Children's Health. Retrieved June 21, 2022, from https://kidshealth.org/en/parents/adhd-school.html

ADHD in the Classroom | CDC. (2022a, April 19). Centers for Disease Control and Prevention. https://www.cdc.gov/ncbddd/adhd/school-success.html#ref1

ADHD in the Classroom | CDC. (2022b, April 19). Centers for Disease Control and Prevention. https://www.cdc.gov/ncbddd/adhd/school-success.html

Low, K. (2008, December 10). *8 Simple School Strategies for Students With ADHD*. Verywell Mind; Verywell Mind. https://www.verywellmind.com/help-for-students-with-adhd-20538

Melinda. (2018a, November 2). *ADHD and School - HelpGuide.org*. HelpGuide.Org. https://www.helpguide.org/articles/add-adhd/attention-deficit-disorder-adhd-and-school.htm

Melinda. (2018b, November 2). *Teaching Students with ADHD - HelpGuide.org*. HelpGuide.Org. https://www.helpguide.org/articles/add-adhd/teaching-students-with-adhd-attention-deficit-disorder.htm

School changes - helping children with ADHD | CDC. (2021, November 29). Centers for Disease Control and Prevention. https://www.cdc.gov/ncbddd/adhd/features/adhd-and-school-changes.html

5 Ways to Indulge in Some Self-Care - Kalos Medical Spa. (2019, October 23). Kalos Medical Spa. https://www.kalosmedicalspa.com/5-ways-to-indulge-in-some-self-care

Amy. (2018, December 26). *15 Self-Care Strategies for Parents*. Verywell Family; Verywell Family. https://www.verywellfamily.com/self-care-for-parents-4178010

Burton, N. (2020, November 2). *Self-Care Strategies for Parents When You Have No Time for Yourself*. Healthline; Healthline Media. https://www.healthline.com/health/parenting/self-care-strategies-for-parents-no-time

Felman, A. (2020, July 8). *Take Care of Yourself: 25 Science-Backed Self-Care Tips*. Greatist; Greatist. https://greatist.com/happiness/ways-to-practice-self-care

Importance of Self-Care: Why Parents Need Time Out to Recharge - HealthyChildren.org. (n.d.). HealthyChildren.Org. Retrieved June 21, 2022, from https://www.healthychildren.org/English/family-life/family-dynamics/Pages/Importance-of-Self-Care.aspx

The Importance Of Self Care And 5 Ways To Indulge »Read More. (2021, May 18). Daily Mom; http://www.facebook.com/dailymomofficial. https://dailymom.com/shine/the-importance-of-self-care-and-5-ways-to-indulge/

The Importance of Self-Care for Parents | Psychology Today. (n.d.). Psychology Today. Retrieved June 21, 2022, from https://www.psychologytoday.com/us/blog/adolescents-explained/202107/the-importance-self-care-parents

GoodTherapy Editor Team. (9 C.E., Autumn 2009). *Therapy for Parents, Therapist for Parenting Issues.* GoodTherapy - Find the Right Therapist; GoodTherapy. https://www.goodtherapy.org/learn-about-therapy/issues/parenting/get-hel

Parent Support Group Programs - Child Welfare Information Gateway. (n.d.). Home - Child Welfare Information Gateway. Retrieved June 21, 2022, from https://www.childwelfare.gov/topics/preventing/prevention-programs/parent-support-groups/support-group-programs/

Parenting support | Action For Children. (n.d.). Action for Children. Retrieved June 21, 2022, from https://www.actionforchildren.org.uk/how-we-can-help/get-parenting-support/

Parenting Support Group: Top 3 Support Groups for Parents. (n.d.). MensGroup.Com; https://www.facebook.com/mensgroup1.

Retrieved June 21, 2022, from https://mensgroup.com/parenting-support-group/

Support for parents: where to get it | Raising Children Network. (2022, March 28). Raising Children Network. https://raisingchildren.net.au/grown-ups/services-support/about-services-support/services-support

Printed in Poland
by Amazon Fulfillment
Poland Sp. z o.o., Wrocław